ACTIVE
OPERATIONS
MANAGEMENT

THE PLAYBOOK FOR SERVICE
OPERATIONS IN THE AGILE AGE

NEIL BENTLEY AND
RICHARD JEFFERY

First published in Great Britain by Practical Inspiration Publishing, 2021

ISBN   978-1-78860-231-0 (print)
       978-1-78860-230-3 (epub)
       978-1-78860-229-7 (mobi)

Practical Inspiration
Publishing

Contents

Contents

Introduction

It can be tough being a manager in service operations right now. If you are working as a manager at a bank, insurance company, or any other service where you have a number of teams working for you, you might feel beset on all sides.

On the one hand: keep all the lights on the dashboard green – respond to 90% of requests within 24 hours, achieve 100% compliance, improve your Net Promoter Score. You live with centrally established staffing levels while being asked to loan staff to the latest change programme. You have to improve quality, reduce costs, manage risk and compliance, and take on additional work.

On the other hand: improve your Great Place to Work score, explain to a worried workforce how great it is going to be introducing 50 robots or offshoring half the work. You have to cope with more or less work arriving than was forecast, keeping people busy but not overloaded. You have to cope with technology problems (without making excuses) and deal with the consequences of people going sick or leaving to work elsewhere.

And if there were another other hand, you are probably also dealing with a greater-then-ever pace of change: implementing new services, using new technologies, maybe employing some 'robots', and maybe even fundamentally changing ways of doing business.

If this sounds familiar to you, if you sometimes feel that running the operation really ought to be easier, then you are not alone. We have met and worked with thousands of people like you and we are here to tell you that there is a better, easier, way. There is a way of feeling more in control, being able to quantify and manage that endless sense of 'business', and a way to release the full potential of everyone who works for you.

We have been researching, implementing and improving our approach to running operations for nearly 20 years now. The method we have developed, and will introduce to you, is called Active Operations Management (or just AOM). If you adopt this method, you will be in good company. The idea of AOM, as a method for running back-office operations, has grown in influence over that time. What started with a few 'early adopters' in the UK has now spread to be a global practice. You will find AOM being practised in more than 30 countries. It may already be in use in parts of your own company, somewhere in the world.

In this book we will share our experiences and show how you, too, can simplify the task of running your operation. We will cover:

- Why it has never been more important to pay attention to the way you balance work and capacity and how much better things can be if you do.
- What to pay attention to in order to make changes work and last.
- How to plan and manage your resources in a radically simple and engaging way.
- And, in the post Covid-19 era, with digitization and automation at the heart of delivery strategies, what the future holds for operations.

Operations tend to be led by pragmatists rather than theorists so this is a book about a practical method that has been demonstrated to work many times over. It is designed to help you make a difference on the ground. We have tried to keep it lighthearted and easy reading while introducing you to some of the background thinking behind why it works. We will share worked examples, case studies and stories from our many years of working with some fantastic clients.

As well as being action oriented, we take a very people-based perspective to improving the management of operations. Many technologies help with the planning and scheduling of resources in operations environments (you are almost certainly using one or more of these already) but most of these come at the problem from a purely technical, even mathematical, perspective. The people who work for you are treated as part of the problem: a cost to be monitored, optimized or automated away.

We start with the people. Customers are people who need a service, the people who work for you deliver that service and they, in turn, are managed by people. And all these different people have their own strengths and weaknesses, hopes and fears. Even with the increasing digitization of work in service operations, running an operation is still a people-based challenge. We have put people – the customer, you and the people who work for you – at the heart of our method.

Will it work for you?

- The approach has been successful across thousands of diverse operations and processes, independent of geography and cultural context, in the public or private sector, with 20 years of use cases, refinements and developments.
- You almost certainly already have many of the features and elements for success in your operation today, as have so many of our clients over the years. What is universally true is the power of coherence and consistency in operations management. Our method has provided the guiding structure for many organizations to truly embed a culture of excellence in professional operations management, rapidly and sustainably.

If you are tired of fighting fires or managing from one crisis to the next; if you want to feel in control of events rather than at the mercy of them; if you want to lead a happier and more engaged bunch of people, then pick a starting point, dive in and read on.

How to use this book

Not everyone reads a book the same way or wants to get the same things out of reading it. We have tried to reflect this in how we have structured this playbook. The four parts of the book cover the following questions: Why? What? How? What next? Although there is a logical sequence and you can easily read the book from cover to cover, you could also dive straight in to the practical 'how to…' stuff in Part 3 and maybe come back to the why and what questions later. Here is a very brief guide to the different parts of the book to help you decide where you want to go first.

Part 1 talks about why it is important to have a method for operations management. The pace of change is greater than ever and a sound way of managing takes away a whole lot of unnecessary variety. It also creates a solid platform from which it is much easier to manage change.

Part 2 explains what we mean by AOM and sets out the ideas and principles behind the practicalities of the method. If you are the kind of person who wants to know why something works, rather than just trust that it does, you may want to read this before Part 3.

Part 3 will be the likely starting point for any arch pragmatists who just want to get on with things. This is the *how to do it* part with flow charts, case examples and suggested methods. This is the heart of the playbook.

Part 4 looks up and out and offers you a chance to reflect on where improving operations management fits into the other changes that will be going on around you. It also discusses the likely implications of some current industry trends. If you are grappling with robots or getting used to a more home-based workforce, you will find some useful ideas in this part.

However you choose to read this book, we hope you find it thought-provoking and helpful.

We have also placed a number of resources online for you to access. You can find this toolkit at https://activeops.com/aomtoolkit. Feel free to dip into these if you want further practical guidance on making AOM work for you.

SCAN FOR TOOLKIT

Part 1

The importance of having a method

This first part deals with the question of 'why': why you need to read this book and why having a method for simplifying the running of your operation will benefit you, the people who work for you and the organization that you work for.

In Chapter 1 we show why we think your role, and that of people like you, is so important. We talk about the scale of service operations and the pace of change that is likely to be going on around you. We suggest that it is more critical than ever to have a simple and effective method for staying on top of the day-to-day challenges.

Chapter 2 gives more detail about what we mean by service operations so that you can relate what we are saying to your own work. We also explain how service operations are unique and need their own solutions – not just borrowing ideas from manufacturing or project management.

Chapter 3 introduces you to the AOM method and explains how some very simple changes can help you to achieve real and lasting benefits.

Chapter 4 goes into more detail on the benefits of AOM for you and others and will help you to make the business case for implementing AOM.

Chapter 1

Why this and why now?

Anhera's story

Some while ago, while working in New Zealand, Richard was due to meet a team leader who had recently implemented a new management system that was being introduced across her organization. Anhera ran the mail room and every day dealt with the hundreds of mailbags delivering and dispatching the materials, correspondence and forms of the organization.

Richard took a breath and steeled himself for what he thought could be a challenging encounter. Anahera had a reputation for no-nonsense straight talking. An imposing Maori woman, she was utterly committed to her role. It mattered to her that her team sorted and dispatched the items to the right place because she cared about her customers, just as she cared for her team and how they felt at work. Not uncommonly for this function in organizations, she had mostly junior staff, often in their first job. She was the quintessential mother hen – fiercely demanding but also utterly committed to their wellbeing.

How would Anhera respond to the introduction of our AOM system?

As they met, it was obvious something was up: she was agitated and emotional, verging on tears. Richard braced himself as she started talking.

> For the first time in my 15 years in this role, I feel safe and in control. My team members are going home knowing they've been successful. I'm having proper discussions with my peers about our work and who needs help, and we've been able to

stop Saturday overtime, which has been a problem forever. It's transformed my life.

As Anhera continued, Richard began to relax:

Until now, we have always been the problem area, or the bottleneck: never mind people going sick, unexpected mailshots, big events or policy changes bringing torrents of work, we still have to get the work done by deadlines that stayed the same – and there was always a background pressure to reduce costs and raise performance.

I was always on the threshold of a nervous breakdown because I felt we were just waiting for the next crisis to hit. No one ever says thanks for being on time – but I feel terrible when we're behind but also frustrated and angry for my team when it's outside our control.

Today, all those uncertainties around work volumes, staff absence and the myriad of other factors which make running operations such a challenge *are still there*. But now – for the first time – I feel in control of my responses to those challenges. I know with confidence where I am and what I am going to be tomorrow and next week – to a level of confidence that we feel safe. Safe to rotate my team to develop them in new roles, safe to make commitments to other team leaders to loan or borrow resources, safe to have adult conversations with my managers about resource requirements and productivity improvements that I can see being available.

By now, Richard was joining Anhera in feeling emotional as she became more and more animated.

And it has transformed the lives of my team – because now they are a critical part of the process of knowing what's going on and what we need to achieve. Rather than just waiting to be told which fire to jump to put out or scanner to operate, they know their contribution and impact on the business and our customers.

As she finished, and feeling slightly overwhelmed by the emotion being expressed, Richard reflected on how the reaction of this one woman in one team crystallized everything that he and Neil believed in and hoped for from their work. This showed that among all the talk of productivity gains, business targets and strategic goals, there is a human side to operations. There is a choice about the way we manage ourselves and our teams, and it doesn't have to be reactive and stressful.

Anhera's story is about one person and her team. It is about making an impact on success, job satisfaction and achievement among the relentless pressures and constraints of running modern operations. Today, there are thousands like her who have discovered the difference *being in control* makes to themselves and to the people around them.

If you recognize the challenge and pressures of operations management Anhera described, and would like to make a difference to your own working life and those around you, we wrote this book for you.

Of all the books, on all the shelves, in all the stores, you had to look into this one

There must be millions of books on management so why pick this one? Is this the one? Will this be the book you read rather than just put on the shelf? Let's be honest: it isn't likely to be the one you leave lying around on the coffee table to impress guests at your next soirée, but will it be the one you recommend to colleagues? Will it have dog-eared corners and bristle with sticky notes in a few years' time for repeated reading?

We hope so, of course, but that rather depends on whether we are addressing a real need for you. Did Anhera's story resonate with you?

Would it be good to feel more in control? We will start by setting out our stall so that you can decide now if you should move on or read on.

This is a book all about service operations. That is to say, the part of the organization that delivers the goods to customers in businesses like banks, insurance companies, shared service centres and the like. You might call it operations, or the back office, or customer services, or 'just the thing I need to do to pay the mortgage for a few more years'. If you manage a team, or a number of teams, that processes information and delivers services to customers then this book will have something to offer you.

We are going to talk about Method: an approach to planning and managing the resources you have (mainly your people, but maybe some robots too) to meet your customers' needs. Method: really? You're doing this every day of your working life; what can we possibly teach you? That is hard to say since we haven't met you but we hope our opening story illustrates that even talented people who care about their operation can sometimes benefit from a fresh way of looking at things. Anhera was a good team leader working in a well-run operation but still found real benefit in a new method.

It is not that managers aren't running their operations well, but like any capability or skill, the challenge is to improve, to refine and probably most importantly to be consistent, over time and with others, to achieve the very best performance. Many operations are run very well but often organize themselves very differently: between geographies, departments and even between teams. It is this lack of consistency that embeds limits on how well service operations are run. This is as important if you are running just a few teams in a larger operation as it is for whole enterprises, or for the service operations sector as a whole.

Why should others get all the good methods?

Millions of people all over the planet work in offices providing some kind of service to customers – many with telephone headsets on, many more sitting at computer screens. They might be part of a process for underwriting someone's mortgage, or processing an insurance claim; or they might be working in one of the vast number of business processing outsource (BPO) services – such as payroll, accounting, HR or customer relations.

The machines that these people use don't make a lot of noise; they don't hiss or steam and generally don't make things that you can touch and feel or stockpile in warehouses. And yet many of the management methods that have been applied to the people working in these 'service operations' have come straight out of the world of manufacturing. Indeed, the types of operations we have worked in for many years have often been referred to as 'clerical factories'.

We think this is unhelpful. Although we can learn lessons and adapt principles from other business sectors, service operations deserve to have theories and methods of their own, which work with the grain of their unique features. In particular, service operations are people operations. In this book, we intend to describe methods that have been designed from first principles to suit this world.

Have you noticed how many books, blogs and advisors seem to draw on other disciplines when trying to show you how run your operation? Have you seen books on operations that are almost exclusively about manufacturing? Or seen consultants talk about how Lean manufacturing could be applied to running a bank? Or how Agile software development could show you a thing or two about improving customer service in insurance claims processing?

Have you ever wanted to shout back: 'But we don't make widgets!'? Or something similar?

If you have, you can be assured we are writing for you. This book does draw on decades of the best thinking in management, but our single mission is to make this relevant to, and work for, people who work in service operations.

All too often, 'operations' seems to have been a forgotten discipline. It doesn't have the same qualifications as accountancy, the same standards as project management or the same airtime as PR or marketing. But the work that you do is every bit as valuable as these other disciplines; it is a professional discipline that should be recognized and valued. We are working on that. In certain sectors in Australia, you will now find job adverts specifically asking for evidence of accreditation in AOM. Many companies are adding AOM skills to their competence profiles and evaluation frameworks. This may not yet be the case in your business or your country but you can still benefit from learning the method that is becoming a must-have approach for many similar operations to yours.

It is big and it is important

Just to remind you that you are part of a big movement, let's consider just how important your sector is.

According to the International Labour Organization, just over 50 million people worldwide work in financial and insurance activities. Of course, not all of these people work on the kinds of transactional processing activities that we talk about in this book, but many are. That is just one sector of the economy; many other sectors also have high levels of service. Even in sectors like manufacturing, many people work in offices processing orders, managing accounts, creating customer experiences, handling human resources demands – rather than laying hands on metal. Yes, service operations is huge, global and vital to modern economies.

We are talking about a significant proportion of the working population of the world. Significant enough for it to be important that the operations in question are run efficiently and effectively. Take as an example one sector in one country: banking in Africa. This is close to our hearts as we have both loved working in Africa where our South African-based team has worked with many of the region's major banks. The number of people with a bank account and who are using banking services has risen from 170 million in 2012 to around 300 million in

2017 and is set to reach 450 million by 2022. That is a lot of customers and a lot of customer service transactions.

This may not matter to you as you drag yourself out of bed on a wet Wednesday in winter, but you are part of a big and important thing. You, and everyone involved in service operations, deserve the very best.

It's the people, stupid

It was Bill Clinton's 1992 presidential campaign that ran with 'the economy, stupid' as one of its key messages. In service operations we think it is worth adapting this to remind ourselves that people are at the heart of everything we do.

How well service operations are managed can significantly influence the health and wellbeing of the people working in an organization. You can have a big influence over creating a healthy and happy climate for the people who work for you.

You may have heard of contact centres being referred to as modern-day 'dark satanic mills', alluding to the challenging nature of some of these workplaces. Of course, it is a bit of a stretch to suggest that the pressures of working to tough call volume targets or to strict call handling times would be anything like the unhealthy and exhausting nature of the work in the mills of the Industrial Revolution, but it is fair to ask if the best of modern management theory is being applied to the modern working environment.

It is not just us who have pondered this. Professor Andy Nealy, founding director of the Cambridge Service Alliance and a Fellow of the European Operations Management Association (among many other grand accomplishments), wrote in a paper with Bernard Marr:

Evidence in the literature suggests that performance management in call centre environments missed the evolution seen in the field of general business performance management since the beginning of the 20th century right through until today...[1]

The professor goes on to suggest that much of the management of contact centres is based on old theories of Taylorism, or scientific management, relying on outdated command-and-control mechanics such as time-and-motion study, quota setting and the like. We think this is true in much of the world of performance management in service operations (not just in contact centres), and the problem is that the human dimension is being underplayed at best, or overlooked entirely.

All of this despite it being commonly accepted that a well-motivated and engaged workforce will be far more productive than an alienated and disaffected one. We also know that wellbeing at work has become a hot topic. Here are a few facts listed in an article from *Personnel Today:*[2]

- 1.5% of the working population suffers from mental health issues (Source: *Health & Work Strategy – Work-Related Stress*, Health and Safety Executive, 2017).
- Mental health accounted for the loss of 11.7 million working days in 2015/16 (Source: *Health & Work Strategy – Work-Related Stress*, Health and Safety Executive, 2017).
- 30.8 million working days are lost due to back problems and suchlike (Source: *The State of Musculoskeletal Health*, Arthritis Research UK, 2018).

---

[1] B. Marr and A, Neely, 'Managing and measuring for value: The case of call centre performance', Research report for publication by Cranfield School of Management and Fujitsu, 2004.

[2] 'Promoting workplace wellbeing', Personnel Today, 10 October 2018. Available from www.personneltoday.com/hr/health-shield-promoting-workplace-wellbeing/ [accessed 9 September 2020].

- Poor mental health costs UK employers between £22bn and £42bn each year (Source: *Mental Health and Employers: The Case for Investment*, Deloitte, 2017).

We believe it is self-evident that people at work should be treated as adults who will give their best endeavours to the organization they work for if given the chance to do so. Creating a management system that puts human beings at the heart of the system as opposed to treating people as just another operational problem to be managed is not just the right thing to do, it is good business sense.

Why this and why now?

We are finalizing this book while under lockdown in the 2020 Covid-19 crisis. Organizations have had to pivot, almost overnight, to new models of working with nearly all their staff working from home. Organizations have been finding out the hard way where, far from 'data-based decision making', operations management actually relied on subject matter expertise and being able to see the teams and the work. Not easy when all members of your team are now home working!

But even before Covid-19, the world around service operations was changing very fast and this, we would argue, makes the case for having the best possible method for running the operation. Running the operation, day to day, needs to be as natural and effortless as breathing so that you can focus your attention on the myriad changes and challenges that are hurtling towards you.

Work is being done faster than ever and customers expect speedier response times. This shortens your time to think and respond and adds to the demands on your planning and control systems.

The way work gets done has become more complex. Think about your own environment: is all the work done in one office? What proportion of the work done to serve a customer is done by people all employed by the same company? How much of it is outsourced, or off-shored? How much of the work is actually done by people now, or are some of the people being replaced by robots?

It doesn't stop there. Over the years, we have seen operations get increasingly complex. Here are a few more head spinners:

- New channels: in the branch, by phone, email, online. The way the work arrives keeps changing.
- Greater customer sophistication: customers expect more, make use of comparison websites, have better pricing information.
- Market disruption: some new companies are completely redefining whole sectors.

In offering you a method, we aren't addressing all of these issues for you, but we are showing you a way of giving yourself, and the people who work for you, more time and mental space to deal with these. Many of these may be 'above your pay grade' as they say but as sure as night follows day, they will end up at your door. If you are worrying about yesterday's backlogs, or today's service-level agreements, it is hard to find time to consider tomorrow's transformational change. We can help you to find the time.

People are the solution to be set free, not the problem to be contained

AOM is an approach to managing service operations that puts people first. Even in a 'digital-first' world, the customers are still people, and much of the work done for those customers will still be done by people, who in turn are managed by people. Operations management is still a human equation and, in many ways, increased automation will, in turn, place a greater emphasis on empowering people to use their creativity and ingenuity to deliver great service to customers. This will only happen if the management systems are built on the assumption that our people are the solution to be set free, not the problem to be contained.

It is not always easy to make something simple: it has taken us years of research, learning from every client we have worked with, absorbing any literature we could on many different aspects of leadership and management. This is what we have distilled into this book: our method, AOM.

The AOM method is based on a process for collective time management – planning and managing the 'raw material' of service: time. We will show how you, as a manager, can support your teams in achieving greater levels of control, capacity and choice over what they do, by establishing common standards and definitions which enable teams to co-operate and make work more flexible and agile.

We will now go on to look at service operations like yours in a bit more depth and explain some of the ways your challenges are unique.

Chapter 2

The nuts and bolts of service operations

What we mean by operation and operations management

In Chapter 1, we argued that service operations represent a big and important part of the global economy, and the work that you, and people like you, do affects the quality of working life for millions of people. Unsurprisingly, we are not alone in saying there must be a better way – your operation won't be short of people looking to offer you help, advice, new methods and new gadgets. Many of the solutions that have grown popular in organizations like yours have their roots in either manufacturing practices (such as Lean) or project management disciplines (such as Agile). In this chapter, we will explain some of the unique features of service operations so that you can see how a solution that is designed specifically for your world will be the best for you.

There are three parts to this chapter:

1. What we mean by operations, service operations and Service Operations Management.
2. The unique features of service operations.
3. The things that make your operation different to other operations.

The aim is to help you make informed choices about how to improve the management processes and practices in your own world.

Operations: Where the rubber meets the road

Operations are the part of an enterprise that produces the goods or delivers the service to the customer. It is the function that delivers on the enterprise's promises; it is where the rubber meets the road.

At its simplest, we could think of a service enterprise as having the following functions:

The bit we are talking about is 'Deliver it'. Maybe the enterprise is an insurance company. New insurance products get designed (think of multi-car insurance, for example). The product is developed with clever underwriters making sure the risks make sense and then the product is launched and sold. The core of the operation involves activities such as signing up new people to the policy, administering those policies over time; managing changes of details, renewing premiums and so on, and then also handling claims made against those policies.

For us, this is the core of the operation and is typically the element of a business that we will work with. Essentially, we are looking at a simple process:

Obviously, the customer satisfaction process can involve many other processes – some being very people intensive and others completely automated. What matters is that operations involves the activity of satisfying customer requirements.

Now, just to add a little complexity, if we think about 'internal customers' it is possible to think of functions such as Finance and Accounting or HR as also having an operations function within them. The rise of shared service centres and business process outsourcing has crystallized this. Often, very large operations are entirely dedicated to serving these functions. All of this says that, one way or another, operations are all around us.

Service operations

We talk about service operations to differentiate from other uses of the word 'operations'. The term operations has particular meanings in computing, retail, manufacturing, as well as hospitals, so we need to narrow this down.

The service sector is huge. It could mean anything from a hairdresser to a hotel, a physiotherapist to a psychic healer. Service is also what we expect from our banks, insurance companies, the tax office or the welfare system. The term 'service operations' is generally reserved for these second examples because these typically involve large numbers of people carrying out high volumes of transactions. The work is generally information-intensive and the people are working in a front office (communicating directly with customers) or in a back office (processing information which is then communicated out to customers). If you work in an office with many tens or hundreds of colleagues, organized into teams, delivering services to many thousands of customers, then this book is for you.

Service Operations Management

By *Service Operations Management*, we mean the set of activities that contribute to making sure that the operation delivers what its customers want on time, at a satisfactory quality and acceptable cost.

This involves organizing people (and machines) into a series of teams and departments, and then co-ordinating their efforts to deliver the best outcome. Some aspects of managing the performance of the operation are very people-centred: engaging, motivating and directing people; while other elements are more technical: forecasting demand patterns, scheduling resources and managing work queues. Both people-centred and technical aspects are important.

Taken together, the disciplines that make up Service Operations Management have a massive impact on the efficiency and effectiveness of an enterprise. Now we need to look at the ways in which the unique features of service operations are going to guide you towards a very specific type of operations management system.

Unique features of service operations: The four '–ilities'

If you search for 'service characteristics', you will pretty quickly come across the following four features:

1. intangibility
2. inseparability
3. perishability
4. variability.

We are not really sure who to credit this to but it is very widely 'out there'. If you ever find yourself in one of those situations where someone says to you something like: 'it's a bit like in manufacturing where…', you can stop them and say: 'no it isn't'. Service operations are unique. Your world is unique: the better you can describe what makes it different the easier it will be to implement workable solutions that will give lasting benefits.

Let's take a quick tour of the '-ilities'.

Intangibility

Very often, a service is actually carried out by a member of the staff for, or in the presence of, the customer. No goods change hands; there is nothing for the customer to touch and feel. 'Yes, the money will be in your account on the 6th' could be a very satisfactory end to a service transaction, but you can't park it outside your house and polish it like a new car.

Many services in banking, insurance, tax assessment and so on involve information exchange. (As an aside, this is why the associated processes are coming under a lot of attention from robotic automation.) You can't stockpile information in the same way you can goods in a factory. You can't have an inventory of mortgage 'sub-assemblies' waiting for an order to come through. Most work in services has to be done just in time to meet immediate customer demand. This idea of Just in Time has become part of the language of Lean or Toyota, but in services it is a necessity rather than an innovation. Services out of necessity work 'to the heartbeat of the customer' – it isn't something that needs to be taught. This in turn means that you can't keep people busy by working ahead of demand. If the work dries up, people become less productive. It's not their fault; they just don't have stuff to do.

Inseparability

In a similar vein to intangibility, quite often you can't separate the customer from the service. As someone put it at a conference Neil attended a while ago: 'You have to be there to have your hair cut!' This is certainly true in contact centres (as well as hairdressers) where the customer is on the other end of the phone.

You can't 'scrap and rework' a bad phone call in the same way you might a faulty component. If an agent is rude on the phone or sends out incorrect information in an email, then the error is immediately in the hands of the customer.

This puts huge emphasis on getting things right first time. Making errors and then trying to recover from them can cost a fortune. The implication for Service Operations Management is that time needs to be made available to prioritize prevention over cure. Give people the time and resources to get things right first time: make sure people are trained, capable and motivated.

Perishability

No, we haven't started talking about fruit and veg here. Service is perishable too: an agent's words on a phone call or a notification sent to a customer in an email have a very brief shelf life.

Services often cannot be stored: they happen in the moment. This has especially big implications for service. You cannot be certain of meeting demand by building a warehouse full of ready-made mortgage acceptances so you have to ensure that you can respond to demand when it arises.

People now expect almost instant answers to anything but the most complex of transactions. Meeting that level of service expectation can be expensive. You can only go so far rationing service supply to match your workforce by building queues. If you want to always be able to respond instantly, then you need to have sufficient resources to deal with peak demand – all of the time. By simple logic, this means that you will have a lot of unutilized resources most of the rest of the time.

Supplying a perishable service very responsively is inherently inefficient because it requires holding onto resources just in case of a surge in demand. Later we will show how you can blend different services together to keep the overall operation efficient while still being responsive where necessary.

Variability

The very nature of interacting with customers, people talking to other people, brings a level of variability to the 'product' that would not be countenanced in a manufacturing environment. A machine might make a certain type of widget at a rate of 100 a minute with a tolerance in fractions of a second. One person making a car insurance claim might be off the phone in five minutes while another will be determined to tell the agent everything from make of the car that hit them to the car's suspiciously bulging front near side tyre that probably accounted for it swerving into them. No two interactions will be the same.

This has profound implications for resource planning and trying to predict how much time you will need to get all the work done. The idea of a 'standard time' to convert work into resource requirements has a long history in work study but its application in service operations has often been naive and simplistic. If the insurance claims agent feels they have to take 20 minutes to process each claim, they will have an impossible task. On the other hand, it might be reasonable to budget that 30 claims might on average require 20 minutes each, meaning that it makes sense to set aside 10 hours to process 30 such claims – allowing for the anticipated variability. The point is that time can be budgeted to give agents the space to do their job, but it should not be used to micromanage every minute of their day.

That's the four '-ilities'. These are a useful way to make sure that your approach to operations management is right for your world of service operations. Next, we need to consider that not all service operations are the same. How can we assess what makes your world unique among other service operations? We need to look at the four Vs.

What is it like in your world? The four Vs

Do you have very high volumes of work like retail banking maybe? Or perhaps your volumes aren't so high: wealth management perhaps. Do you have a variety of products such as general insurance or are you highly specialized in something like equine insurance? How variable is your work? Very variable could be an operation delivering unemployment benefit, which fluctuates according to many social and economic factors. Not so variable might be administering a 'closed-book' investment scheme. Finally, how visible is what you do to the customer? Does it matter if the work is done in the next hour, or minute, or second, like a contact centre? Or do you just need to get stuff done 'behind the scenes' and the customer won't really notice?

The four Vs: volume, variety, variability and visibility define your world and have a big influence over what your operations management system should look like. (Full disclosure here, we should say that we didn't think up the four Vs. We learned about it from Nigel Slack, a leading Professor of Operations Management whom we met through Warwick Business School.)

Put simply, if you are thinking, 'Well I've got high volumes, a lot of variety, everything varies from day to day and what I do is really visible to my customers…', then you have come to the right place. If you are big on all the Vs then operations management cannot be left to chance. Having a method to help you to simplify and control your world will make a huge difference.

The eternal triangle

We will conclude this chapter by looking at what you probably have in common with almost every other service operation: targets. Understanding the way in which business targets interact and affect decision making is key to understanding what your operations management method should look like.

Let's just check:

- Are you constrained by costs? Do you have to work within a budget? Every operation we have worked with have had to live within cost constraints. This has been true of profit-making businesses, public services and charities. You may not have a target to drive down costs and increase profits, but chances are you still have to work within a budget.

- What about quality? Does it matter if the work in your teams is reliable, accurate, compliant with internal procedures or industry regulations? Almost certainly. Everywhere we have worked has had a requirement to do things right, give the customer what they need, comply with regulations and follow company protocols to minimize risk to the organization.
- And service? Do your teams have service-level agreements? Most operations have targets for how long customers should wait for a response. Sometimes these are highly public commitments and other times simply internal standards. Either way, they can have a big impact on how you plan and manage your resources.

Together, cost, quality and service interact with each other to make improving all of them quite a challenge. Which of these is currently keeping you awake at night?

We often depict these in our work as being like electrons buzzing around a nucleus. The idea we want to convey is that these are three essential components but also that they are vibrant, changeable and, crucially, interrelated.

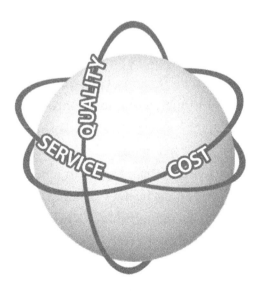

Let's take a look at how these three components affect each other.

First, what does it cost to improve service? Improving responsiveness to customers will generally add cost. If you work in a contact centre, you will know that answering 90% of calls in 10 seconds is going to cost more than answering 80% in 20 seconds. The same is true if you are responding to emails or 'snail mail'. To be more responsive, there has to be someone available to do the work and so improving service generally means employing more people, even though some of them may not be fully occupied all the time.

What about quality? Does it cost more to produce higher quality? Often the answer to this is no. It is cheaper to get things right first time than to get them wrong and then have to fix them. In many instances, getting things wrong leads to a lot of extra work. This extra work is even given its own name: *failure demand*, and this can be as much as 50% of the work done in some operations.

It might cost you extra to do more training or to make sure people don't rush their work, but as both of these things improve quality they will almost certainly pay you back many times over.

The complex and dynamic relationships between cost, quality and service can make it hard to manage collectively; the result can be an endless game of chasing your tail. Imagine the scene:

First, you have an out-of-the-blue bad customer satisfaction rating and a new quality programme is launched. Time is diverted into training and 'customer focus' sessions. Unfortunately, this costs money in the short term (even though it will save more later) and so budgets get squeezed. Recruitment is slowed down and overtime is discouraged. This results in service levels being missed because not enough staff are available. A different Twitter Storm begins to emerge and so an edict goes out that service levels must be hit. Corners get cut, work is rushed and people work late even though there is no overtime (which isn't great for morale). Now quality starts to suffer… and so the story goes.

Getting out of this vicious cycle requires making some time for yourself, but how do you conjure that up out of nothing? The good news is that AOM can help you to do this. It can help to release time that is lying dormant in your teams at the moment and turn it into useable time; this can kickstart a positive cycle of improving service, preventing quality failures and easing pressures on cost so that more can be invested in further improving service and so on.

Happiness is getting a balance between cost, quality and service. The next chapter will tell you how AOM can achieve this.

Chapter 3

How AOM helps to achieve balance

In 2013, one of our clients mentioned that on a top consultancy firm's training course she learned about managing performance using something called the *Red Bead Game*. Neil's first reaction was to question why a modern consultancy would still be using such an old teaching game. He probably hadn't thought about that game in nearly 30 years but as he reflected further, he recalled that this game probably planted the seeds of one of the core principles of AOM: that, more often not, opportunities for improving performance are found in the way people are working, rather than in the people themselves?

The game was invented in 1982 by Dr W. Edwards Deming, the man who taught the Japanese and then Americans all about quality. You can actually watch a YouTube video of him teaching the game although we hesitate to recommend it because at 38 minutes it is pretty tough watching.[1] Instead, here are the spoilers.

The game involves volunteer workers from the audience 'producing' white beads. They do this using a special paddle with 50 holes in it that they dip into a container that has a mix of white and red beads. As the workers pull out the paddle, the red beads are counted as quality defects and the white beads as good production. Depending on what the facilitator wants to teach, various performance management techniques are used to try to improve the performance of producing white beads.

---

[1] 'Red Bead experiment with Dr. W. Edwards Deming'. Available from https://youtu.be/ckBfbvOXDvU [accessed 9 September 2020].

Workers are told that their job is dependent on producing white beads. Targets are set for the maximum red bead count: workers who produce fewer red beads are rewarded while those who produce too many are threatened with losing their jobs. Visual controls are put on the walls, workers are ranked in league tables, and so on.

Target setting, incentive schemes, forced ranking of individuals, motivational speeches... In short, every kind of individual performance management technique is brought to bear while it is obvious to everyone that this is entirely futile. The number of red beads scooped out of the container will be a matter of pure chance.

Our client described how, playing the game, she experienced a slow, boiling frustration – which was of course the point of the game. If people were rewarded for success, it was actually just good luck that they scooped only white beads. Or if people were punished for producing red beads, this was a performance over which they had no control. Poor production was being treated as a result of poor attitude when there was nothing any individual 'worker' in the game could do about the mix of red and white beads.

People's performance is often more limited by the opportunity to perform well than by their willingness or ability to perform. How can you give people that opportunity to be the best they can be?

The importance of opportunity

Deming said: 'The fact is that the system that people work in and the interaction with people may account for 90 or 95 percent of performance.'[2] He was railing against what he saw as misplaced management methods that focused on trying to manage the individual rather than understanding that every person was constrained by the system in which they were working. In particular, Deming was critical of

---

[2] Deming quoted in P.R. Scholtes, *The Leader's Handbook: Making things happen, getting things done.* McGraw-Hill, 1998, p. 296.

methods that set quotas for individuals or that set targets for people that were outside of their direct control.

Too often we have seen incentive schemes, target setting and gamification (where people win 'badges' and such like for 'good' performance) that seem to imply that performance would improve if only everyone tried a bit harder. The reality is often that these mechanisms are introduced into an operation where the things that really constrain performance are not the people themselves, not their attitudes or their abilities, but the way they are organized and managed.

For that reason, we like to stress the following formula:

Performance = Willingness × Ability × Opportunity

This performance formula is fundamental to the way we have designed our AOM method. Multiply high willingness by high ability and by *zero opportunity* and you get zero. In this chapter, we will talk about how to give people the opportunity to perform. We do think that managing people according to their willingness and ability are important and will return to this in later chapters. First though we have to address the third part of the equation since it can quickly cancel out the other two.

Focusing on opportunity is why AOM achieves such dramatic and lasting benefits in very short order: it gives people the opportunity to be the best they can be. It doesn't try to change them, or make any assumptions about them; it takes people as they are and then allows them to perform to the best of their abilities more of the time.

Measuring how much more teams could achieve compared to what they currently do on average gives us an estimate of *latent capacity*. We need to get into some detail around latent capacity because this is probably the fastest and most sustainable performance improvement you will ever make.

Latent capacity

This is a very important idea and will be covered in a lot of detail later in this book so at this stage all we want to do is give you a quick introduction. We are covering it here in the context of explaining why we say that AOM will rapidly deliver greater performance and improved control. The technicalities of how that is achieved we will return to in Part 3.

You might find the example we use here trivially simple, or it might involve more mathematics than you ever cared to see; either way, please stick with us. This concept gets to the heart of how AOM can deliver such positive improvements in performance and we are introducing it now so that you have a good idea where the benefits of AOM come from.

In its simplest terms, AOM delivers better performance because the potential for better performance is already there. It is latent, sitting at the desks and walking the corridors of your building. The people in your teams, serving your customers, can very probably deliver more. But this is not to criticize your people in any way at all. Rather, it is to wonder at the untapped potential and to ask how we can get out of people's way and let them be as good as they can be. You can find some more guidance on calculating and interpreting latent capacity for your own teams in your online toolkit at https://activeops.com/aomtoolkit.

What Deming was telling us in his Red Bead Game was that it is generally not the willingness or ability of the people that limits performance; it is the system that they are working in. Improve the system and you will release the latent capacity in the people.

Safe Hands Insurance

We will illustrate what we mean by latent capacity with a simple, fictional example. The Claims team in this made-up company has ten people carrying out the work. Each can process, on average, ten claims a day. The team has capacity for 100 claims a day, or 500 a week.

To keep things simple for now, let's imagine a week in which everyone turns up for work every day. No sickness and no holiday. What can we learn from looking at the workflow for a week?

	Monday	Tuesday	Wednesday	Thursday	Friday	Totals
Claims received	80	110	50	90	100	430
Claims processed	80	110	50	90	100	430
Number of people	10	10	10	10	10	50

Two days are of particular interest. How did ten people manage to do 110 claims on Tuesday? We said their capacity was only 100. We can assume for now that they either rushed the work or worked late to get it finished. Wednesday stands out because less work was done that day than the team were capable of doing. On this day, the team's productivity was very low. Ten people did the work of five because that is all that was available to be processed. We say that the productivity is 50% because 50 claims were processed compared to a capacity to process 100.

The team were half as busy as they could have been, but clearly this does not mean that the people had become lazy overnight, or lost their motivation, or had forgotten their claims handling skills. Of course not. The issue is one of opportunity. They could have done more work but the work was not there to be done.

It is common to see high levels of productivity as critical to managing costs and remaining profitable, and so we might reason-ably consider Wednesday 'A Bad Day'. Maybe it was, but we certainly shouldn't blame the people doing the work. We can't say the people were lazy that day or performed poorly. It was not their fault that they didn't have sufficient work to occupy all ten of them.

Looking back, we can see that the way to have achieved higher productivity would have been to move five people out of the team. Then the remaining five would have been fully productive and the transferred five could have done something else useful for the wider operation.

Clearly, looking back is no good. The time has gone and you can't get it back. But, and here's the important bit, what if we had been able to predict in advance a little more accurately how many claims were likely to come in and then only schedule just the right number of people to do the work?

Looking at the week as a whole, the team had capacity to process 500 claims but only processed 430. That is all that were available. That would give a productivity value of 86%. But what if we were able to move some people in and out of the team? We could see the following picture:

	Monday	Tuesday	Wednesday	Thursday	Friday	Totals
Claims received	80	110	50	90	100	430
Claims processed	80	110	50	90	100	430
Number of people	10	10	10	10	10	50
Loan/Borrow people	-2	+1	-5	-1	0	-7
Actual people deployed	8	11	5	9	10	43

This shows that we could get all the work done but with fewer people over the course of the week. We loan out eight days' worth of time over the course of different days but also borrow someone for a day on the Tuesday so that we don't have to stretch people too hard.

The difference between the scenario where we have a team of ten people doing the work irrespective of the volume of work to be done and the scenario where we *actively match* the number of people to the amount of work shows the potential to release a net seven days to be productive elsewhere in the business. We now have a team with capacity to process 430 claims over the week and 430 claims to be processed, moving our productivity from 86% to 100% – a 16% increase in productivity.

So here we have latent capacity in a nutshell. Actively matching the resources used to the work to be done releases capacity that can be used in other ways in the operation. Doing this routinely in a systematic way that involves and engages everyone in the teams creates a lasting increase in capacity, which can be translated into improving service, implementing change, reducing cost or whatever else the corporate priorities dictate.

So, what is the routine and systematic way of releasing this capacity? As we have already said, you can't go back in time to make use of the capacity that went begging on any given day so there has to be a forward-looking approach. It is simply this:

1. Forecast next week's workload as best you can and then plan to use just enough resources to do that amount of work. Plan to borrow some resources from elsewhere if you can to cover any peaks in workload and plan something else of value for people to do when the workload drops.
2. Monitor how this goes very closely each day, and during the day, to make sure things go according to plan.

While you can rarely get this spot on, you can turn a large amount of what would otherwise be lost time into useful work. No one is being asked to work harder than they are able (in fact, we try to make sure that they are never overloaded like Tuesday in the above example) but more can be done by making smarter use of the time.

What about the real world?

What happens in your teams if you find that you have too much or too little work for your team? In our simplified example, we showed how you could balance by lending staff to other teams or borrowing from them. You may be thinking that this would not be possible in your own environment because of specialist skills and system access restrictions, but in the real world we see operational teams solve these problems and lend and borrow around 10% of their resources.

Lending or borrowing is only one of the available possibilities. You may be able to adjust the schedules of your part-time and temporary staff, use overtime, build up or eat into work in progress[3] or change the amount of time on other activities such as projects, training or one-on-one coaching sessions.

This is clearly a very simplified example so you would be forgiven for asking if it works like this in the real world. The answer is an emphatic yes. We could show you hundreds, thousands probably, of Excel spreadsheets with tables and charts showing this effect in operations worldwide. This is because we carry out this latent capacity analysis as part of the health check we do with any new customer. We also give customers the means to monitor this for themselves on an ongoing basis.

Of course, the real world is much more complex. Not only will the amount of work coming in vary, so too will the number of people available to do it. Added to that, you might have backlogs of work carried over from previous days and will almost certainly have many different tasks to perform, not just one, as in the Safe Hands Insurance example.

For illustration, here is a real image of a chart from a client health check that shows how productivity fluctuates in line with the volumes of work received.

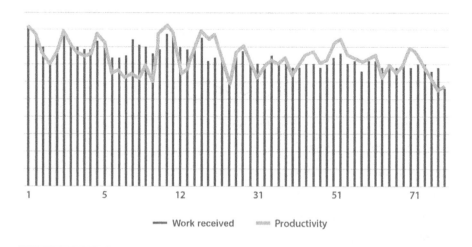

— Work received   ▬ Productivity

---

[3] Work in progress refers to work that has been received for processing but is not yet complete. We tend to call this *work in progress* if the work is still within service-level targets and *backlog* if it is outside service level.

You don't need to worry about the scale in the diagram; all you need to note is that the line links up points of daily productivity. The peaks are days when people were very busy (too busy maybe) and the valleys are days when things were relatively quiet.

This has all occurred because the amount of work coming in and the amount of people available to do the work both vary and are not synchronized. When available time is high and incoming work is low, productivity is low. When available time is low and incoming work is high, people are working their socks off.

Implications of fluctuating productivity

Hopefully you can see that if you were to find this sort of fluctuation in your own team it would represent an opportunity. With some simple forward planning, you could make use of time available on the low-productivity days and also make sure that you avoid, as far as possible, overloading people with too many high-productivity days.

There are, in effect, free resources waiting for you to tap into. It doesn't need a new investment in robots, or offshoring your operation. Nor does it need insightful process improvement programmes or inspiring leadership programmes. All of these might be very helpful to you, and give you even greater gains, but the quickest and easiest gain is just sitting there waiting for you to take it.

But, despite the clear benefit of making better use of quiet time while not over-working people at other times, we still find people arguing that surely this is just natural variation. People have argued with us that variation is harmless, inevitable, or even that it is a good thing: you have a busy day, so then you have a quiet day to recover. Surely variety is the spice of life? It might be if you are choosing a holiday destination, but in a working environment, variety is an absolute killer. Here are just a few reasons why.

Strain on the system

Essentially, wildly fluctuating productivity indicates a system that is out of control. The peaks in productivity probably indicate periods of overload. Not all work is getting done and service is suffering. That, or people are working beyond their capacity, cutting corners or getting tired and quality is suffering. Meanwhile, there are periods where time is being used ineffectively and costs are higher than they should be. The problem is that if you simply cut costs in this uncontrolled environment, then the overload strains will only get worse, ultimately adding back even more cost because it is always more expensive to fix errors than it is to prevent them.

Trying to implement any significant change when the basic system is out of control is likely to lead to cost overruns, missed benefits and generally disappointing outcomes.

Strain on the people

Perhaps even more important from our perspective, fluctuating productivity puts strain on people. By way of an analogy, fuel consumption in cars is often presented as both urban cycle and motorway. The start, stop, accelerate, brake of the urban cycle is much less efficient than running at a smooth 70mph for a couple of hours.

The same is true with working environments. Rushing, waiting, rushing, waiting is as much a strain on a team as it is on a car. It isn't efficient and can be hugely stressful. Working at a steady pace might sound boring, but is far better than the alternative. Psychologists talk about 'flow' when people are doing something that they find challenging but doable. Time passes more quickly and people feel energized and fulfilled. Sports psychologists sometimes call this 'getting in the zone'.

Fluctuating productivity is stressful in another way: it represents a state of not being in control. Imagine working in an environment where you don't know when you wake up in the morning if today is going to be boring or busy beyond a joke. Variety might be the spice of life, but only if you have some choice over that variety. And here is the point: one of the biggest causes of workplace stress is the feeling of not being in control. Stress comes from feeling like a victim in an uncertain environment, or feeling like those 'up the management chain' have no handle on things. Stress comes from having no say, no control.

Losing the signal in the noise

Looking back at the chart of fluctuating productivity, you may see that it looks like a noisy sound wave and, in many ways, it is very much like that. With all that 'chatter' it would be very hard to pick out one important sound. Likewise, with endless days of high and low productivity it would be hard to identify what a good day actually looks like. This has an impact on planning and on evaluating performance improvement projects.

Imagine trying to estimate the benefits of automating a process, or even trying to choose which processes would be best replaced by RPA (robotic process automation). With all that fluctuation, how would you pick a benchmark? Imagine if a process improvement had been implemented and one task was simplified to take 80% less effort. Would you even notice the difference among all that noise?

You will see as you continue through this book that stabilizing productivity is vital to creating a platform for change. Until you take this self-inflicted variation out of the system, it is very hard to see the opportunities for improvement, make the business case for them or extract the benefits from them.

The five principles of AOM

What we have discussed so far leads us to the principles on which AOM is founded – the five behaviours of successful operations managers. These simple phrases exemplify the culture of AOM and provide the basis for the detailed design of the methods that we will be explaining in Part 2.

The diagram below summarizes the five principles, contrasting traditional operations management with the AOM approach.

Traditional Operations Management	AOM	
Functions are over-staffed 'just in case' something goes wrong.	**Use it or lose it**	Work and resources are matched 'just in time', delivering service with efficiency.
'Quality is important to us, but could you just rush this one?'	**Actions speak louder than words**	Words and deeds are matched because the operation is in control.
Get as good as possible at fixing things when they go wrong.	**Prevention is better than cure**	Get as good as possible at preventing things from going wrong.
Plans are something you do for the boss, if required.	**Keep plans in sight and in mind**	Plans are something you do to help you to help your team.
Strive to meet the targets, but make the targets easy to meet.	**Strive for the best possible outcome**	Stretch yourself and your team to get better.

Use it or lose it

This refers to using or losing time. If you don't use time in the moment, it is lost forever. Unused time just disappears, while unfinished work stays with you.

The traditional approach to staffing has been to overstaff in order to meet service levels, to avoid building up backlogs of work, and to cope with all those 'just in case' scenarios such as receiving more work than planned, someone calling in sick, or the work being more complex than expected.

It is important to have sufficient resources to guarantee responsiveness and to meet tight service levels, but this doesn't mean that excess time should be wasted. In AOM, the right amount of time required to do the work is scheduled for when it needs to be done to meet customer demands, thus maximizing productivity, while allowing any additional time to be put to good use elsewhere in the operation.

Achieving this relies on forward planning and good feedback loops. It is no good looking back at the end of a week and saying: 'That would have been a good week to get some training done.' The AOM method will show you how to produce plans so you can quickly and easily make use of all available capacity and not waste any of it.

Actions speak louder than words

The challenges in managing the triangle of competing demands mean that traditional managers are often caught in a bind. For example, they might say that quality is all-important but then appear to be encouraging people to rush work to meet service-level targets.

Team members often find themselves trying to interpret mixed messages and it is not entirely surprising if this leads to confusion, cynicism or defensiveness. This can't be good for the operation. We believe the best answer to driving out unintended mixed messages is to improve day-to-day control of the operation so that it is easier to match deeds to words.

We don't mean 'control' in the sense of top-down, dictatorial 'command and control' of the employees (far from it). Instead, we mean improving control over the operating environment, creating a management control process with planning and feedback loops that make it easier to stay in control and avoid being buffeted by events.

Prevention is better than cure

This is perhaps most closely associated with managing quality. It is better to spend time and money getting things right first time rather than spending even more time and more money on having to find and fix faults. But this part of the AOM philosophy goes much deeper than that. Here are just a couple more examples where prevention is better than cure.

Staff attrition. It is much more costly to run constant recruitment and training programmes than it is to invest in creating a climate that increases the chance of retaining staff. AOM helps to create a calm, controlled environment that supports front-line staff and helps them to be great at their jobs and to feel more connected to the work of the operation. A small investment in more disciplined planning and control pays dividends in staff loyalty.

Customer service. Failed service, just like failed quality, leads to increasing costs. Miss expected service levels and you get additional enquiries chasing the work. Make a customer feel rushed or give them an incomplete response and you get follow-up letters or complaints. Poor customer service leads to more work, which then leads to greater risk of delivering poor customer service.

AOM helps you to schedule resources to give you greater confidence of hitting service levels first time every time without bankrupting the business. You don't have to trade efficiency (by overstaffing) to guarantee service levels. That is a very traditional management view of the world. You just have to create the right blend of work and resources.

Keep plans in sight and in mind

As John Lennon said: 'Life is what happens to you while you're busy making other plans.' While it is true that events rarely turn out as planned, traditional management often uses this as a reason either not to plan, or to ignore plans and just react to events.

Reacting to events is stressful, tiring and costly. Rather than letting plans slip out of sight, out of mind at the first sign of trouble, AOM encourages you to use plans as your navigation aid. You can see how far you have been blown off course and figure out what it would take to get back on course.

In AOM, plans are not a stick to beat people with; they are a means of creating a supportive and collaborative environment in which everyone has a voice and everyone has a purpose.

Strive for the best possible

So much of traditional management is about setting and measuring targets that trying to hit them risks becoming a manager's main focus. We all know that targets are a means to an end (customer service), not an end in themselves, but it doesn't feel like that if your annual bonus is dependent on hitting those targets. Of course, once hitting a target becomes the main goal, it is logical to then focus on negotiating the easiest target possible.

Out of this is born the well-worn tradition of negotiating targets or budgets. Budgets are 'sandbagged' in the certain knowledge that the finance director will take a knife to them. The finance director takes a knife to budgets in the certain knowledge that they have been 'sandbagged'. (Sandbagged may be a specifically British English term. We heard the use of the term 'hollow logging' in Australia to describe a similar process – other cultures probably have their own imagery.)

What you will see with the AOM philosophy is an emphasis on using clean, clear data to calculate realistic targets and not just leave it to negotiation skills. With this comes a further emphasis on getting better and better. Setting and meeting targets, yes, but always looking for the optimal, not the merely satisfactory.

The AOM universe: five key principles

So far in Part 1 we have been building a case for a new approach to Service Operations Management. One that is built to deal with the unique challenges of service, that solves the problems faced by service operations and is founded on modern management behaviours.

In Chapter 2, we said that cost, quality and service represented the three requirements of all service operations. Now we are going to add these five principles to our picture to show them around the three interacting elements helping us to take control.

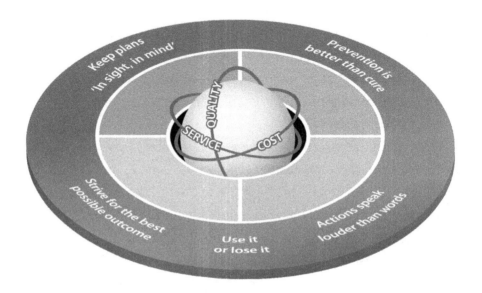

Chapter 4
Why bother?

Any change involves investment. That investment is likely to include cold, hard cash but it will also involve putting in time to make the changes, and spending a certain amount of 'political capital' as you stick your neck out to say 'trust me, this is worth doing'. For this reason, we feel we should arm you with the reasons why you should bother with AOM.

If you have read this far (and not just opened the book at a random page) then you have already put in some effort. Now we will spell out why it will be worth your while continuing.

Everything in Part 1 of the book has been building up to this chapter. In Chapter 1 we made the case for finding a better way to manage service operations. We suggested the need for a method that built on the unique nature of service and didn't just try to force-fit manufacturing or project management methods. Chapter 2 unpacked that special nature of service a bit more, setting us up for an under-standing of what kind of management methods would work best in this environment. Chapter 3 then explained how you can use AOM's capacity planning to release latent capacity and gain control.

But what would increasing control and releasing latent capacity do for you?

What's in it for you will depend to some extent on exactly what your role is. As we said at the start, we are assuming that you are either a department manager, leading a number of teams, or you are a change agent supporting such a manager. In this context, we can summarize the benefits as follows:

- For you: an easier life with fewer surprises. You will find it easier to meet your 'balanced scorecard' targets such as efficiency, service, risk/quality and employee engagement.
- For the people who work for you: a greater sense of belonging, less stress and better wellbeing. And the benefit for you here is that it is so much easier to manage happy teams.
- For the company you work for: increased efficiency, greater adaptability and increased competitive advantage – all of which will make your job more secure and satisfying.

These are bold claims to make, so we had better set about justifying them. First, we will summarize what it is about AOM that delivers these benefits and then we will go into more detail on how AOM will benefit you, your teams and your organization.

Capacity, control, choice

Okay, so it isn't quite 'Peace, Bread, Land' or 'Liberté, Egalité, Fraternité', but this is our rallying cry. This is how AOM delivers benefits.

First, capacity. As we saw in the previous chapter, AOM releases latent capacity by helping you to make better use of the time available in your teams through forward planning and good operations control. If you implement AOM, you will nearly always see increased productivity but that is not to say that productivity improvement will always be your primary goal. It will however give you the capacity to get your work done with fewer resources, or to do more work with the resources you have. In our experience, almost every operation we have worked in has had a laundry list of things they would do 'if only they had more time'. AOM will help to find, and use, that time.

It is true that the time made available could lead to simple cost cutting but it is much more common to use it to do more, and greater, things for the business.

On to control. We explained that most operations have wildly fluctuating productivity due to constant mismatches between the amount of work to be done and the resources available to do it.

As soon as you start to get really good at matching work with resources, everything becomes calmer and more controlled. As we will see, this sense of being 'in control' rather than buffeted by events is a huge source of benefit at all levels within the operation.

And choice. The choices you make or that your business makes will always be limited by constraints. Time and money are finite, priorities have to be devised and choices made. Releasing capacity and improving control, as described above, free up some of the constraints and give operations a wider range of choice. Of course, many of the choices made may be higher up in the organization – things such as introducing new products or automating some work with 'robots'. But at least you may have more choice over when and how these things get done and feel less forced into having to prioritize between serving customers and introducing big changes.

More on this in a moment, but suffice to say that choice, and the agility to act on the choices made, is critical to the long-term competitive advantage of your operation. Ultimately that is what keeps you and everyone who works for you in the job.

Let's now take a closer look at how the 3Cs of capacity, control and choice can benefit you.

The 3Cs and you

We can't know for sure what your working day looks like. We have probably never met (assuming someone outside of friends and family actually reads our book) but we have met many hundreds of department managers, team leaders and change agents working in service operations and have found similar patterns all around the world.

Regarding capacity, we rarely find a department manager who couldn't use some extra resources. Imagine, for example, that AOM helps you to achieve a 20% improvement in productivity (not, we must stress, by working people 'harder' but just by making the best possible use of time available). What would you do with the equivalent of one free person for every five you employ?

That capacity, combined with the greater control that AOM gives you, will mean a quieter life for you. Targets will become easier to hit and, when things are more challenging, at least there will be fewer surprises. You will have had a good early warning as to what was coming down the track and the time to prepare to deliver the best outcome under the circumstances.

Over time, AOM will develop your team leaders into great leaders, working with a common method and shared tools so that it is easier for you to know what is going on. That knowledge, and your team leaders' growing capability, will improve trust and let you delegate more responsibility into your teams, giving you time to look to the longer-term and wider business issues. Now wouldn't that be a refreshing change?

The 3Cs and your team

Releasing capacity can be an understandable worry for people working for you. Two things are always a concern: first, are you just going to make people work harder? (No, on the contrary, people will feel under less pressure if we manage time very effectively.) Second, are there going to be job losses? We can't answer that one for you but all we can say is that in almost every case we have seen, capacity released through productivity gain has been used to do more for customers, to grow the business and to make the business more sustainable for the long term. If businesses really need to cut costs, then sadly that sometimes involves job losses. We hope that never happens, but even if it does, it is better that it is done in a controlled and measured way so that the business can stabilize and recover. AOM can help with that if necessary, but it is rarely the driving reason for doing AOM.

It is most likely that releasing capacity will give people greater opportunities for training and development and for broadening their roles. In a world where automation and artificial intelligence are beginning to be implemented, it is vitally important that human workers receive opportunities to develop their skills for working on the complex, or customer-facing, work that is less well suited to robots.

The word 'control' can be a double-edged sword in the world of operations. It can conjure up images of the outdated method sometimes called 'command and control' where people are treated as brainless and idle production units who will only work if forced to do so. This is not what we mean at all. When we talk about control, we are talking about being in control. That is to say, not being buffeted about by events, uncertain of what is coming next. This has significant benefits for wellbeing at work. Studies have shown that one of the major causes of stress at work is not feeling in control. Anything we can do to help people feel just a little more control over their daily working lives is going to pay great dividends.

We have seen many operations turn their corporate noses up at flexible working, remote working and suchlike because they feel that they will lose control of the work. As operations gain greater control, they can start to see the real benefits of increasing flexibility, broadening people's skills and giving them a greater say over when, where and how they work. When you feel confident you can offer your team members flexibility without losing productivity, you'll find them more engaged, happier, and less likely to call in sick.

The 3Cs and your company

Businesses have to look for a bottom-line benefit, and AOM must be able to justify its implementation in real economic terms. We have seen four distinct types of business case for doing AOM. These centre around whether or not the sponsoring executive is looking for short- or long-term gain and if they are focusing only on the core operations function or looking at how the operations function contributes to the wider business.

These considerations and decisions may be outside of your control but we will include them in our discussion because there is always a chance that if you become enthusiastic about implementing AOM, you may have to make the case to the finance director or CEO as they decide which projects to prioritize.

Let's take a closer look at those two perspectives that we just mentioned:

1. Time frame: shorter or longer term. Is your company looking to make a difference very quickly to achieve a clear and urgent outcome, or can it afford to take a longer-tern view that AOM is an investment in your overall business capability?
2. Focus: operations or enterprise. Clearly, AOM is an approach to operations performance management but is your company looking solely at the operations function, or is it interested in the wider, enterprise, benefits of having a great operations function?

Taking these two perspectives, we get to the four categories shown in the following diagram.

- *Problem Solving*: short term, operations focus. This is the category if your business is looking to address a specific need such as 'we need to reduce the cost of overtime.' This could cover an immediate problem in any of the KPIs – cost, quality or service. If your business fits into this box, the business case is likely to be fairly straightforward. You are looking for a direct improvement in performance and so you should be able to quantify this as a financial gain and specify a direct return on investment (ROI).
- *Standardizing Operations*: long term, operations focus. If your company sees itself in this box, the emphasis is still on

'operations for operations sake', but not so focused on an immediate pressing need. It is not so much that any one part of the
operation is performing poorly; rather, there is a belief that the
whole of the operations function could perform better if it all
worked to the same standard model. We have found that this
is a common motivation among business process outsourcing
organizations or where corporate shared service centres need
to standardize.

Here, short-term improvements in the performance of individual business units will be a bonus – and will help to under-
write the cost of the initiative. The anticipated benefits are
more long term though, based around the common methods
simplifying reporting standards and enabling greater degrees
of integration and resource sharing.

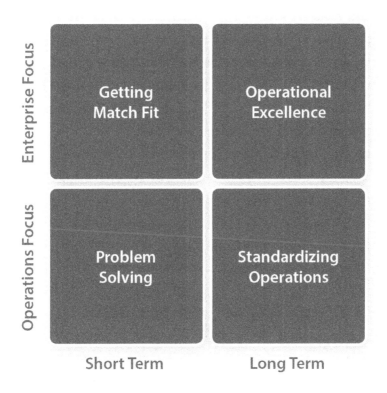

- *Getting Match Fit*: short term, enterprise focus. This is one of the most common motivations for getting involved with AOM. The emphasis here is on the third C: choice. AOM helps organizations to get the best out of their other strategic change programmes and it is in this sense that we use the term 'Match Fit'. Think of it as getting ready to take on big changes. We could also have used the term 'Agile' here as this has gained popularity recently to talk about businesses that are good at responding to or delivering change.

  AOM will help if your company is looking at competing with new challenger outfits in its market, or is looking to introduce new products or channels to market, or is maybe considering introducing robots to the workforce. In every case, AOM will release capacity to support the change process, and will improve control so that benefits can be estimated, measured and realized.

- *Operational Excellence*: long term, enterprise level. This final reason for taking on AOM is a bit further out on the visionary scale. This is simply about wanting to be excellent at running the operation because this is a good thing. Sometimes a business decides to implement AOM because it believes that doing operations better than anyone else in their sector will lead to competitive advantage. This effectively embraces all three of the other boxes described above: becoming more efficient and removing local problems, standardizing across the enterprise on one best way, and becoming more agile so as to be able to respond more rapidly than the competition to changing markets.

  People often associate certain organizations with how well they run their operations. Toyota is famous for its production management methods (a lot of which we have adapted to work in service businesses); General Electric is famous for pioneering the Six Sigma approach to managing quality. These are companies that have enhanced their reputation for being able to deliver by explicitly pioneering a method for managing. With AOM, maybe you could help your company to become the 'Toyota of banking' or the 'GE of insurance'.

Summary

The benefits of AOM come from the 3Cs of *capacity, control and choice*. These offer benefits in different ways depending on your point of view. We cover this from the perspective of a department manager, a member of a front-line team and a senior executive.

	Capacity	Control	Choice
Department manager	Effectively assign extra resource to get the work done. Everything becomes a little easier.	No surprises. Better contingency planning. Improved service standards. Reduced operational risk. Improved staff engagement.	Easier to delegate, allowing the department manager to look forward more strategically.
Team members	Less pressure at peak times, more time available for development.	Greater input into how things get done. Less stressful working environment. More pride in the performance of the team and company. Happier customers.	More likely to be able to work flexibly to the employee's advantage.
The company	Capacity for change: more able to take on strategic projects.	Control over benefits: more likely to be able to estimate, measure and deliver benefits of strategic projects.	Greater choice of strategic options as a result of improved capacity and control.

At the company level, the benefits of AOM typically fall into one of four categories: problem solving, standardizing operations, getting match fit and delivering operational excellence. At the personal level, following AOM will mean happier and more successful teams, and a quieter and more predictable working life.

We hope we have done enough to convince you to read on. In Part 2 we will explain a lot more about what AOM is and why it will work for you.

Part 2

What is AOM and how does it work?

Now we are going to lift the lid on the AOM method. We will tell you what it is and where the ideas have come from. We are not going to ask you to simply follow some management recipe: we are going to explain to you why it works. Knowing this will help you to make AOM work for you.

Chapter 5 introduces the idea of systems thinking. This is a way of thinking about organizations that will help you to plan and implement changes that will make a lasting difference.

Chapter 6 explains how we have taken systems thinking into the AOM method to come up with a four-part framework for you to use to plan your operations improvement.

Chapter 7 focuses on the people side of the operation you lead. It talks about the behaviours and the skills required to run great operations.

Chapter 8 focuses on the organizational side of your operation. It talks about shared methods and the tools to support those methods.

Chapter 9 will give you a chance to do a little self-diagnosis and compare your operation to AOM best practice.

Chapter 5

We are all out of magic bullets

When we first went to Australia to start to build our business out there, we were lucky enough to be able to spend some time at weekends exploring this wonderful country. We heard a story, with which many people will be familiar, about the problems that they have with cane toads in north-eastern Australia. This is a wonderful cautionary tale about how a finely balanced ecosystem can be disrupted and about the unintended consequence of human action. It is relevant here because simplistic change in organizations can have a similar damaging effect. Here's the story.

In 1788, Australia started to grow sugar cane. By the early part of the 20th century, they had a big beetle problem. Cane beetles and French beetles were causing havoc to the crop and, when conventional pesticides had not solved the problem, the country looked for an innovative solution.

In June 1935, cane toads were introduced into Australia by the Bureau of Sugar Experiment Stations. This turned out to be a failure of epic proportions. First, they didn't control the beetle problem. The toads couldn't jump high enough to eat them. Second, with no natural predator in Australia, the cane toad just became a new pest.

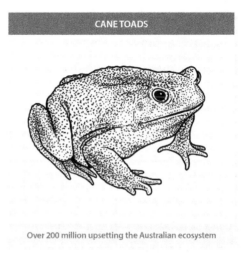

CANE TOADS

Over 200 million upsetting the Australian ecosystem

Around 100 young toads were released in the Queensland area in 1935, but there are now *over 200 million toads* in north-eastern Australia and, according to Wikipedia, the cane toads were migrating at a rate of 37 miles per year in 2014. We heard tales of Queenslanders being encouraged to run over them and of 'Toad Day Out' events where the poor animals were collected up and killed.

The toads have caused great damage to the Australian ecosystem. Native predators have died eating the poisonous toads. Good news for crimson finches who are doing great since monitor lizards have died eating the toads when they should have stayed on a finch-only diet. Native plants have suffered and so too have some insect species, leading to some insect-eating animals going hungry. You get the idea: one change; massive knock-on effect.

The story of cane toads illustrates the law of unintended consequences. It is what happens when we interfere in complex ecosystems. We can probably all list other examples, such as the introduction of myxomatosis to control rabbit populations in the UK, or the effects of deforestation on not just ecosystems but also climate systems.

What does all of this have to do with operations management?

Our point is that organizations are like ecosystems. Both are a complex balance of interdependent elements, and simple changes in an organization (such as introducing a piece of new technology, a new process-mapping project or a cultural change initiative) can destabilize the balance of the elements and either fail to achieve its objectives or actually do more harm than good.

It seems like management teams everywhere are always looking for the next magic bullet to solve all of their problems, and management consultants are often only too happy to oblige. But these magic bullets will rarely work with the complexities of the real world.

Next time someone comes to your operation offering a magic bullet solution, ask them cryptically: 'or is this just another cane toad?' They will probably think you are mad, but you'll know what you mean.

***

In Part 1 of the book we were trying to persuade you (or help you with the arguments to persuade your bosses, co-workers and subordinates) why it would be a good idea to take on board and implement the principles of AOM. In doing so we have hinted at what AOM is: a method for managing service operation or, more specifically, an approach to balancing the work to be done with the resources available to do the work. Now we want to get into a bit more detail about the thinking behind the AOM method, what it is and why it works.

Part 2 will help you to make AOM work for you, and for your teams. Whether you are leading a small back office in Berkshire, England, or a running huge shared service centre in Sydney, Australia, AOM will work for you. But you will have to work at it, tailor it and make it fit with your own unique culture, structure and systems. AOM is no more a magic bullet than any other big idea or management method. We can't tell you what to do on a wet Wednesday in March when three of your best staff are absent and more customers than ever before seem to have decided that now is the time to enquire about their policy renewal. We have no idea how you should deal with Colin from Accounts who hasn't been himself since his goldfish died. We can give you principles and insight that will help you to approach these issues and any other slings and arrows of outrageous fortune in an 'AOM way'. For this reason, we are going to explain some of the guiding principles behind AOM. We believe that if you know *why* AOM works then you will be more likely to work out *how* AOM can work for you.

In the rest of this first chapter in Part 2 we are going to introduce one big idea. This is the foundation on which the whole of the AOM method is built. The idea is called *systems thinking* and we hinted at this with our cane toad story. Grasp this idea and you are well on your way to being an AOM expert.

Systems thinking

We started this chapter with the story of cane toads to show you an example of a system, and how we humans often seem to mess them up. With climate change, worries about deforestation or having sufficient food for the global population, we are all pretty familiar with the notion of ecosystems: complex interactions between the many living things such as plants and animals, predators and prey, and so on. The cane toad story shows how unintended consequences arise from interfering in a system. The big message we want to get across to you is this: think of your place of work as a *complex human system*.

If you think in these terms, you will generally do the best AOM thing under any circumstance. So let's break down what we mean by each of these three words.

Complex

We use the term 'complex' to mean something that is more than just complicated. Complex suggests a degree of unknowability or unpredictability. If you were to look at a wiring diagram of a Toyota Prius, you might find it somewhat complicated (unless of course hybrid powertrains are your hobby when you aren't reading about operations management). It may be complicated but it is knowable and it is predictable. Someone with the right knowledge could tell you exactly what would happen under any given circumstance.

A modern hybrid-electric car is complicated but a weather system is complex. Even if you are a brilliant meteorologist, you will have to say it will 'probably' rain tomorrow or there is a 'likelihood' of thundery showers. The interactions between atmospheric pressure, the wind, the rotation of the earth and possibly how optimistic the weather forecaster is feeling all combine to give a degree of uncertainty.

Have you heard of the butterfly effect? Not the 2004 movie starring Ashton Kutcher and Amy Smart, but the concept (that the film is based on) introduced by MIT professor Edward Lorenz. His speech to the 139th meeting of the American Association for the Advancement of Science in 1972 was called *Does the flap of a butterfly's wings in Brazil set off a tornado in Texas?*

This idea has passed into common usage and is often misquoted but underneath it is the idea that a small change can have a massive ripple effect as it interacts with other parts of the system. Think cane toad invasions or introducing customer service targets that end up giving customers poorer service. A branch of mathematics has grown up to study complex systems. It is called chaos theory. Now we aren't saying your operation is chaotic (you might think that, but we couldn't possibly comment) but we will bet that it is complex.

Organizations are often complicated, but they are also most definitely complex. There are just so many moving parts. We have interactions between people, working in a hierarchy or structure, with competing demands, and so on. It is not surprising that we often find ourselves talking about 'the law of unintended consequences' where senior managers do something in the organization only to have it backfire on them in a spectacular way. How could they have possibly predicted all the permutations?

The practical consequence of this in the AOM method is that we understand that managers should not try to control everything as though the organization was a series of levers and pulleys (e.g. 'If I introduce this incentive plan, I will get that outcome'). Some organizations try to control everything through one big brain at the top, or through a specialist centralized planning function. This rarely works well. Sooner or later, the complexity overwhelms these centralized controls. The world of organizations, of your organization, is simply too complex. This is not to say that central planning is, in itself, a bad thing. In large dispersed operations it is often very necessary. The right blend of central planning and local control will vary from one operation to the next, but we can be pretty sure that you will benefit from a blend of the two and not from either extreme.

The way to handle complexity is to guide the organization on a journey, responding to changing circumstances as they arise, steering away from trouble whenever it looms. This will become apparent when we get into planning and control in the Part 3. We will show you how to place more emphasis on adaptability than predictability.

Ask yourself how much of your organization is controlled from the centre (or from the top; the two tend to be the same thing in the end). How well does that work out?

Human

Does your organization have any gossip? Are there power plays with people jockeying for position to get a certain role or promotion? Do we care that Colin from Accounts has lost his goldfish? Yours would be a pretty unusual workplace if it didn't have any politics, people issues and power plays. It is simply wrong, in our view, to treat an organization as a mechanical, unfeeling thing or to try to solve everything as if it were a mathematical puzzle.

In some operations, the approach to workforce management (WFM)[1] can focus heavily on the mathematics of the problem and risk overlooking the fact that the workforce in question is a bunch of people. People with hopes, fears, expectations, ambitions and all the other things that make us human. Treating people as factors in a mathematical formula is rarely going to work in the long term, and yet much WFM seems to do just that.

One symptom of this arises when agents try to 'game the system' to improve their performance rating. If you have ever worked in a contact centre, you probably know some of the common 'tricks' that people have tried. Are they bad people or is this just human nature? This sort of behaviour tends to arise when agents have contradictory

---

[1] AOM is an example of a workforce management method – the best example, in our humble opinion.

targets over which they have little or no control (such as 'achieve a 60% sales conversion rate on calls and spend an average of five minutes on each call'). It is simply human nature to try to be in control, so it is hardly surprising that people tend to try to find a way of influencing outcomes that affect them. Particularly if their pay is involved.

Similarly, we evaluated a back-office solution some years ago in which a work manager would 'batch' work up into seven-hour 'bundles' according to a time-and-motion exercise and hand out those bundles for people to complete by the end of the day. 'A day in a day' was the slogan and for some members of staff, the certainty and simplicity of that target was very comforting, while for others it felt patronizing and stifling. With all control taken out of the hands of the people doing the work, there was little incentive for them to show any initiative or innovation. What we saw were human responses to a 'scientific' approach.

The practical application of this to the AOM method is that it uses the disciplines of behavioural science and management psychology to understand things like motivation, politics in the workplace, leadership, wellbeing, and so on. AOM incorporates tools and technologies that work with human nature. In Chapter 7, we will remind you of a few of the basic lessons in leadership, showing how they have influenced the development of the AOM method.

System

'Systems thinking' really is a thing. If you went to a business-school library there would be a shelf devoted to it. You could meet a 'systems thinker' at a party. But if you do, we suggest you talk about football or something (just don't get them started on the weather) as they often have the air of someone who understands the world just a little bit better than anyone else. Systems thinking is important, but it isn't the answer to world hunger or anything. Well, actually, it might be but never mind that. We don't need to go into all the ins and outs, we just want you to be aware of this way of looking at things. To be clear: we are big fans of systems thinking.

In our context, thinking about an organization as a system means thinking about the way the different features of an organization (people, structures, technologies) combine and interact. If you think about your organization as a system, you will be very sensitive to the way changes are introduced and you are much more likely to be successful.

Let's look at this by way of an example. Remember Safe Hands Insurance, our imaginary company? They have decided to reorganize and re-brand. Previously, claims handlers were tasked with recording new claims against a policy and accepting or rejecting claims for cash payments. Under the reorganization, the claims handlers are now 'incident managers' who look after a customer when they make a claim and support that customer through the whole 'claims process'. Think about what has changed:

- The *task* is different: evaluate the company's liability to pay versus support the customer.
- This, in turn, might require new skills, or different *people* doing the work. If you just relabel the people but don't give them any training, or bring in new skills, the initiative is unlikely to work.
- There may be an implication for new *technology*. Safe Hands Insurance now needs a system that can track claims from first phone call to final resolution. Perhaps it also needs to connect to suppliers who provide repairs etc. Again, new technology means new skills.
- It could be that the Safe Hands Insurance *organization structure* would need to change. Maybe smaller teams of incident managers would make sense instead of a large group of claims handlers. That could change the role and skill requirement of the team leaders; it might break up existing working relationships; it might put more pressure on some people to show more initiative and work alone in ways they are not used to.

- Finally, the smaller, autonomous groups of incident managers are likely to have different *control processes:* targets, goals and expectations. These will, in turn, be turned into performance plans and incentives.

Can you recall any changes in your own organization where big change was introduced? It could have been in the task, the people, maybe the technology or the organizational structures or the policies and procedures… How well do you think the knock-on effects of the change were catered for?

So, for an operations management system to work, it needs to take account of the fact that organizations are complex, human systems. Changes will need to affect the way individuals behave as well as the methods that the organization prescribes. Change will require new skills for individuals as well as new tools or technologies for the organization as a whole. Making complementary changes to behaviours, methods, skills and tools represents the AOM way of thinking about the organization as a complex, human system. We will describe these four dimensions of the AOM approach in the next chapter.

Summary

Because we believe that organizations are complex human systems, we have designed our solution to:

- Work with complexity and build control processes that address the complex and unpredictable world of operations.
- Recognize that it is all about people. We take into account human nature. We show you how to think about the effects of what you are doing on the people in your teams.
- Take a systemic view. That is to say, the AOM solution comes at the issues of managing operations from many different perspectives under four headings of *Behaviour, Method, Skills* and *Tools.*

We are now in a position to fill in the last piece of the AOM universe and show you the whole picture.

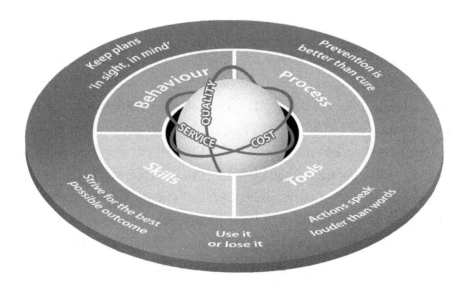

This picture captures all of the elements of the AOM concept.

- We have the three interacting elements of performance that you are always striving to keep under control.
- These are controlled through a management system that has four perspectives which help to ensure that everything you do will lock together to deliver lasting change and isn't just another magic bullet (or cane toad).
- Surrounding this are the five principles of AOM that describe the behaviours and thought processes of all successful operations managers.

That's it, that's the model: it's as easy as three, four, five.

In the next chapter we will talk you through the four perspectives of AOM in a little more detail.

Chapter 6
The four perspectives

Origins of the four perspectives

When we were putting together our method in the early 1990s, we wanted to test ourselves to see if we were covering all the bases. Remember: we wanted to make sure we were influencing the whole system and not just making a change in one or two parts that might then quickly unravel as soon as we had moved on.

Reflecting on what we looked at when we started working with a new client, and thinking about the kinds of questions we would ask, it became clear that there were two broad dimensions to our interests.

Activity   **Capability**

Our first dimension considers what an operation is doing and what the operation is capable of doing. This has always been an important distinction for us. One company might have some fantastic spread-sheets for producing and tracking plans (*Capability*) but then on closer inspection we might find that only one or two enthusiastic team leaders actually bothered to fill them in (low level of activity). In another company, we would find some amazingly good local co-operation between team leaders passionate about getting things done (*Activity*), despite having almost no practical support or infrastructure from their organization (limited capability).

Individual   **Organizational**

Our second dimension looks at the operation as a collection of individuals and also as a collective whole. This is important because the way people behave creates the character of the organization as a whole but the character of the whole organization also influences the way people behave. The two interact and feed off each other. On the one hand, the way you behave with the people who work for you will reflect your values, experience and training. You might be a real people person or get totally turned on by the technical side of your work. Individual differences are important. On the other hand, the way an organization is set up: its reward policies, the tools it uses, what training it gives managers, and so on, are all highly likely to affect the way you and all of your fellow managers behave. Organizational factors influence individual behaviours.

With these two dimensions in mind, we came up with the four perspectives that we now use whenever we look at a new operation. You can see this in the illustration below.

- *Individual Activity*. This is the Behaviour perspective, looking at how people are behaving, what they see as important and how they interact with each other.
- *Organizational Activity*. This is the Method perspective, looking at what kinds of behaviours and attitudes are supported and reinforced by the way the organization expects people to do things. Some organizations have very explicit methods or standard operating procedures, but in many organizations we have found huge variety and what method exists is more implicit than really thought through.

The Four Perspectives

	Individual	Organizational
Activity	Behaviour	Method
Capability	Skills	Tools

- *Individual Capability.* This is clearly the Skills perspective. People's behaviour will be greatly influenced by what skills they have. This is why we often find great team members being promoted to team leader and then performing rather poorly. Their skills are in doing the work so when faced with a team of a dozen dutiful workers all looking for a lead, the team leader is tempted to just take on all the difficult cases for themselves. (Tip: if you want to change behaviours, teach new skills.)
- *Organizational Capability.* The final perspective is Tools. This could be anything from specialist software to home-grown spreadsheets, to the grubby whiteboard behind your desk that still won't come clean since you accidentally used that permanent marker on it. In the same way that if you only

have a hammer you are always looking for nails, the tools that you have are likely to influence the behaviours in your teams.

There you have it: two ways of looking at an organization that give rise to four perspectives. This makes for a satisfying 2×2 matrix that we love so much. The picture looks complete; it feels like all four of these perspectives are necessary to deliver real, lasting change. It also feels like they are sufficient: they seem to us to encapsulate the whole of the system we are interested in and leave nothing out.

We showed them in Chapter 3 as the four parts of the middle ring of the AOM universe; here they are again in the 2×2 matrix, which shows how they fit together and how they relate to each other.

Bringing the four perspectives to life

One of the odd things that has happened to us as our company, ActiveOps, has grown is that now when we visit a client that has implemented AOM it is highly likely that we have not been personally involved at all. Maybe the client did it all themselves, or worked with one of our partner consulting firms, or with our own team of coaches. What this means is that the people in the businesses we visit often don't know us personally and so often they start telling us about AOM as if they invented it (which in some ways they did), putting their own spin on it, and sometimes assuming we don't know much about it.

This is nice because it gives us the chance 'to see ourselves as others see us' or as the poet Robert Burns put it:

O wad some Power the giftie gie us

To see oursels as ithers see us!

To illustrate the four perspectives, here are a few examples of how clients have seen us from one or other of each of these.

Method

Neil once watched a cardboard trophy change hands with much solemnity at a bank in Mumbai when one team displaced another as the current planning champions (the team that was best able to deliver on the plan that they had committed to for the week). They told him that the AOM method had given them greater consistency and certainty. In the past, they had often been unsure what time they would finish the day's work and get on their way home which, given the Mumbai traffic, was a big deal for them. Having a consistent method followed by all team leaders was working well for them. At a lengthy meeting, they grilled Neil on definitions of productivity and various aspects of the theory and practice of AOM. For them it was all about method.

Skills

Neil and Richard have both been honoured to attend passing out ceremonies in Melbourne, Australia for another bank's internal AOM training course. They have handed out certificates of competence to cohorts of around 20 team leaders after listening to a number of them present case studies of improvements that they had introduced into their teams. At this bank, skills and competencies were high on the agenda.

Behaviour

On one occasion, Richard was working in New Zealand while Neil was in Australia. Richard had just heard a senior manager presenting AOM to a different division of a public-sector company. 'I wish we could bottle what she said and how she said it,' Richard said. 'I have never heard the AOM philosophy put across so clearly and passionately.' This has been a common experience for both of us. Many people latch onto AOM as a significant development in the operation's culture and behaviours.

Tools

In South Africa, we have a wonderful client who is always pushing at the technology boundaries. They use the technology that we have developed called Workware™ and they, along with a few other notable clients, are right there at the leading edge working with us on what the technology can do next.

Generalizing from these stories

Of course, the bank in Mumbai didn't just have our method. They used our tools to make it easy to put that method into practice. The Australian bank weren't just teaching any skills; they were teaching the skills associated with using the AOM methods. The exponent in New Zealand who saw AOM as a cultural revolution only did so because the methods, skills and tools all came together to create a new way of working.

These four perspectives form the basis of the diagnostic framework that we will share with you at the end of Part 2 but first are two chapters exploring these in more detail. Two chapters not four we hear you ask? Well yes, we are going to move things along a bit here and bundle some parts together.

First, we will give you a chapter on the individual side of things: behaviours and skills. Second, we will turn our attention to the organizational side and look at method and tools.

As we want to be very action oriented and look at what you can do right now, we will focus mostly on the activity level of our picture – on behaviour and method. The other two are important, but we think that you should define the skills you teach based on the behaviours that you want to see, and that the tools that you develop (or buy) should support the methods that you have established. Behaviour and method drive the agenda and so will get the lion's share of attention from now on.

Here is a map of what is to come based on the matrix diagram.

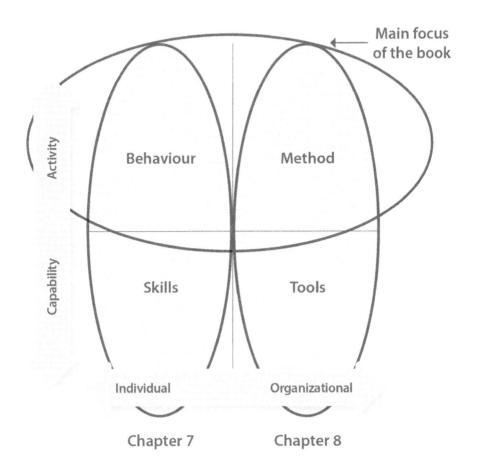

Chapter 7
Behaviours and skills

This chapter is about behaviour, and the skills that support people being able to adopt a certain set of behaviours at work. We will also talk about culture, which is a somewhat overused word in business these days but is nonetheless important. The ideas of culture and behaviour are not quite interchangeable but are entangled. An organization's culture is the values and beliefs that a group of people share and that drive them to behave in certain ways under particular circumstances. Put another way, behaviour is an outward expression of culture. This is important because we are talking in this book about making lasting improvements in performance. You only improve performance by changing behaviour, and you only make lasting improvements by changing culture.

In proposing *Active* Operations Management, we are recommending a certain culture and a certain set of behaviours. So, what do we really mean by 'Active'? Let's have a go at explaining this.

Imagine you are driving across Nebraska in your brand-new Chevy Silverado V8. Not very likely perhaps, but if you were, you would experience General Motors' latest incarnation of Active Fuel Management (AFM). This technology, say GM, improves fuel efficiency by selectively activating or deactivating some of the cylinders to provide the best balance of power and efficiency.

Now imagine instead you are driving your Nissan Micra around the south-east of Birmingham (back in England now, not Alabama) on the M42. Depending on the time of day and the flow of traffic, you will find variable speed limits in place and, at certain times of day, the hard shoulder will also be opened for traffic. The system, which is called Active Traffic Management (ATM… you can probably see where we are going with this!), uses sensors built into the road every 100 metres to monitor traffic flow. The aim of changing the speed limit and the number of available lanes is to create smoother flow: allowing a greater volume of traffic to get through more safely and efficiently.

Last one now. If you sold that big Chevy and invested the $20,000 you made, you might choose to put it into a tracker fund where the value of your investment will rise and fall in line with some pre-determined rules. But if that is all a bit passive for you, you might opt for a portfolio in which the manager buys and sells stocks to try to beat the market. This is called Active Investing or Active Portfolio Management (APM).

So, we have Active Fuel, or Traffic, or Portfolio Management. What do they all have in common? They all use a process of testing what is going on around them and then using this information to make changes to improve the efficiency of their particular system (fuel, traffic flow, value growth). There are constant feedback loops and regular and rapid decision making. Learn and improve, learn and improve. This is what we mean when we talk about *active*.

Active *Operations* Management is another example of this idea in action. It involves constantly monitoring the flow of work and matching people to this (a bit like activating or deactivating cylinders in your Chevy) to achieve the most efficient balance and deliver higher performance and better flow of work, at lower levels of stress.

When systems are complex (like the interaction between fuel consumption and driving conditions, or traffic flows, or money markets), active management is the answer. Rather than trying to set every dial to 'just right' and then sit back and let things happen, active management says keep monitoring and keep tuning the dials. Systems thinking (remember Chapter 5?) encourages, no it requires, active management.

Many operations we have worked with are quick to say that they do this already, and that is often true to some extent. The question is really about how frequently, how precisely, and how effectively. You could drive your Micra economically by being light on the accelerator and coasting down hills, but this is a long way from constantly and automatically monitoring driving conditions to adjust the number of cylinders being used. If we seem to paint things a little black and white from time to time, this is to clarify our argument. In reality, every operation is a shade of grey between the extremes. No operation is completely passive and very few are highly active. But if you can adopt *increasingly* active management behaviours, and encourage them in the people who work for you, our experience suggests that there are serious gains to be made.

Heroes and villains

It can be a bit difficult to really get to grips with culture: the values and beliefs that guide a group of people to behave in a certain way. Lots of organizations talk about culture but achieving lasting change can be very hard. Have you had a culture change programme recently? How did it go?

Results are often mixed and failure (which normally means quietly dropping the programme and focusing on something else after a while) is not uncommon. Part of the problem is that even trying to pin down what we mean by 'organizational culture' can be like trying to nail blancmange to the wall.

To try to help you out, one way into thinking about culture is to think about the types of people that the organization values, how they behave and why is it just what the organization needs or why is it considered wrong and inappropriate? In other words, who are the organization's heroes and villains?

Who are the heroes in your operation? Is it the person who arrives early and leaves late, always seems to have to leave one meeting to get to another as they breathlessly tell you 'I can't stop now; this crisis won't solve itself'? Or is it the one who, with swan-like serenity, sails through the day seemingly unperturbed by anything, but must be paddling under the water because stuff does seem to get done?

Let's take a look at some examples that we have encountered. Please forgive the silly fake names, but it helps us to make the point.

Reactive Ronnie is great in a crisis. When the chips are down and our backs are to the wall, Ronnie can get everyone moving. If we need a backlog blitz, or a quick quality improvement, Ronnie's the guy: he might bust the overtime budget but he'll definitely get us back on track. Sure, he cuts a few corners but the end justifies the means. People are tired but exhilarated in Ronnie's team, and he even buys them pizza if they have to work too late. What a guy!

Hero or villain? Actually, many companies, consciously or subconsciously, place a lot of value on people like Ronnie. People who 'save the day', who always seem to be rushing about, who are always 'putting out fires'.

And here's the thing: when we ask companies to describe their operating culture, probably the single most common phrase that people use is *firefighting*. Talk to front-line staff and they will say that this is exhausting, stressful and that the whole operation feels barely in control; engaged in a constant battle.

Look at this another way and perhaps Ronnie likes a good crisis. It is much more fun (for him) to be standing on the desk being the hero than having a quiet life with all the read-outs showing 'green'. A good crisis focuses the mind: forget everything else, just focus on the problem in front of you. Reacting (and what we are describing here is reactive management) feels easier precisely because it is focused, and if a problem is too big to solve, then your excuses are made for you: no one could have dug their way out of that hole; I did my best.

So much for Reactive Ronnie. What about Bureaucratic Brian?

You might have already decided not to like Brian. The word 'bureaucratic' seems to carry negative vibes. But Brian is a very common species in the management world. He is the human embodiment of the 'standard operating procedure'. He is process and procedure personified.

He works on the basis that no one ever got fired for sticking to the rules. Policy is followed to the letter, particularly if it gets him off the hook. Everyone's good idea is met with the stonewall of 'that's not how we do it round here'.

Flexibility is not high on Brian's agenda. You are not likely to get him to lend you one of his team or persuade him to take on Project X.

Do people like working for Brian? Life is regular, predictable and very different to working for Ronnie. He looks after his staff and they know where they stand. Maybe so, but there is no room for new thinking – procedures don't change (or only very slowly) despite obvious improvements being available. People are discouraged from showing any initiative and may have little opportunity for flexibility or variety.

Bureaucratic management is the second most common form of management we find in operations. It appeals to senior managers who believe that if they do enough analysis and have a strong enough central team, they can be in control of everything. This is rarely the case in the complex world of operations and a fixed rule is often like a stopped watch: it is right, but only twice a day.

Hopefully our childish name calling is helping you to see how certain sets of behaviours can be valued and can start to set the operating culture in stone: maybe a reactive culture, or maybe bureaucratic. Now, before we turn our attention to what constitutes an active culture, here is one last distinction.

What would Passive Percy from Payment Processing say if you asked him how many staff were in his team? Simple: 11.5 ('The half is Emma who is part time and only works mornings'). But if you asked Active Annie from Accounts Receivable, you would get quite a different answer: 'Well, it depends on the day of the week, and even the time of day. I typically need more people on a Monday and fewer on Wednesdays. I also have access to a couple of agency workers that I often use towards month end when things get very busy.'

Active Annie is our hero. She is constantly busy getting things done, and constantly busy making other people's lives less stressful and more focused on the customer. She creates a smooth flow and a sense of calm control, where Ronnie has people bouncing off the walls with stress. Annie is flexible and is open to improvements where Brian's door is closed. Annie works on the system to make people's jobs easier where Ronnie works on the people to make them work harder. Annie *makes* things happen where Percy *lets* things happen.

How many Annies do you have in your operation? The more the merrier!

What makes a good culture?

We have said that we favour active management over passive, bureaucratic or reactive but we need to be careful here that we are not too dogmatic on this point. Brian and his bureaucratic inclination towards following the rules to the letter may well be just what you need in a compliance function, or risk management. When is Ronnie's reactive behaviour firefighting (bad) and when is it being responsive to the customer (good)? Our point is that reactive, passive and bureaucratic often risk drowning out the active management and so this is where we have to pay most attention.

In a similar vein, we mustn't equate active to being over-controlling. We don't want Annie running around like a tin-pot dictator barking orders at everyone. 'Active' is about controlling the situation: staying top of events, not getting on everybody's backs.

We had probably better spell out a few more fundamental values that will help you to achieve an active culture. There are three themes we want to cover here.

1. Attitude towards your front-line colleagues (this might seem obvious, but bear with us, not everyone is like you).
2. Your role as leader – what are you really for?

3. Engaging and empowering the people in your team to do more for themselves so that you will do less (well, different perhaps, rather than less).

Leadership attitudes

One well-known software company with technology that could track the activity of employees from their computer screens ran a publicity campaign on their website under the banner 'Do you know how much time your employees are spending on Facebook?'

While it might be reasonable to expect employees to be doing work, not checking their friends' timelines, we do have some real problems with the implications behind this question and the follow-up sales pitch, which was basically this: 'We can monitor the actions of your staff and tell you how they are spending their time. When your staff are being monitored, they will change their bad behaviours.'

If you have read this far, you are probably with us that this isn't a great management approach, and have a long list of issues yourself, but just to spell it out:

1. The company clearly thinks that this pitch will help them sell their tools. They must be assuming that the managers they are trying to sell to really don't trust their staff and expect them to slack off at every opportunity.
2. They are further assuming that the best way to get employees to toe the line, sit up straight and focus on their work is to make sure they know that they are being watched every minute of the day. That is, as opposed to (and this might seem crazy but...) motivating people to do a great job by getting them to enjoy and take pride in their work. (Just a thought.)

This kind of attitude: that staff are reluctant to work and so must be monitored is an extreme example of what a chap called Douglas

McGregor (Professor at MIT Sloan School of Management in the 1950s) called Theory X. How much Theory X do you have in your organization? Here are some examples of Theory X management:

- High levels of supervision with little employee discretion.
- Employees are given set targets over which they have little input. These targets are set for a short interval and performance is checked often to ensure compliance.
- Rewards are used to encourage people to work harder (such as piece work or bonus schemes).
- Penalties are used to discourage failures to perform.

Remember back to the Red Bead Game that we talked about in Chapter 3? These were all the sorts of behaviours that Deming suggested don't work very well. Why? Because focusing on individual behaviour will generally have a limited effect in comparison to what you can achieve by improving the system that people are working in.

McGregor says that a Theory Y manager assumes that most people would prefer to do a good job given half a chance. The manager's role then is to focus on maintaining motivation and on giving people the opportunity to perform. Give people the time and the tools to do their job and then get out of their way.

Theory Y is our default position, but to be clear: as far as we can tell, McGregor was describing two sets of behaviours, not judging them, and we are not here to judge either. Just to help you consider choices and consequences.

Two other great management thinkers, Paul Hersey and Ken Blanchard, came up with the Situational Leadership Theory, which reminds us to treat people differently according to the situation that you are in. Or put another way: don't tar everyone with the same brush. Imagine you have a very junior and inexperienced team doing a fairly routine task. The kind of Theory X management we described earlier could be entirely appropriate such as setting clear targets and supervising closely. It would be unfair, ineffective and probably very stressful to say to this bunch: 'Yes, go for it. Do as much as you see fit in the time that you work. Take breaks when you think it is appropriate. Good luck, there are lots of other sections relying on you to get this right!' Sometimes telling people exactly what needs to be done and then following up on how they are getting on is absolutely the right thing to do. Equally, it could be very counterproductive to tell your senior underwriters they have to get through five evaluations in the morning before you check up on them to give them their afternoon's allocation. Horses for courses as they say. The right management style for the situation.

Pick a number: how many people do you think in the general population of employable age will come to work and deliberately slack off at every opportunity? Now assume that you have good recruitment policies that aim to avoid hiring the people most likely to offend while hiring those with a good work ethic. Next, assume that you have well-trained leaders and managers who do a reasonable job of motivating the people you have hired. What proportion of people who actually work for you do you think are likely to slack off at every opportunity?

If you think the number is less than half, then you might want to consider where, and how often, you apply Theory X principles. The risk is that some operations treat willing and able workers *as if they are unwilling* and incapable and hence risk them becoming so.

What does this say about the kinds of things that you, or your team leaders, would be doing on a day-to-day basis?

The role of leadership

Managers with a Theory X attitude are often said to manage by command and control: set targets from above (or via a central team), limit individual discretion, follow up regularly, be clear with people who succeed or fail to hit the targets. If this is what you need to do to run your business, then you know that better than us. It is generally right for some parts of some operations but it is rarely right for all parts of any operation, and there is a growing trend at the moment to shift towards greater employee discretion and less direct control. (If you have heard of Agile for example, which is one of the current crop of management methods, then you may recognize this trend.)

So, what is the equivalent to command and control for a Theory Y manager? We call it *coach and co-ordinate*.

In a coach and co-ordinate style, your role (and the role of team leaders working for you) is to create the space to allow people to perform as well as they can. The coach part is a nod towards the world of sport where the athlete 'owns' their performance and the coach helps them to reach peak performance. The coach is facilitating not dictating. The co-ordinate part comes in because, in this culture, you are more likely to be spending time helping teams get what they need (such as borrowing resources from somewhere else, or co-ordinating the sharing of work so that all customers are satisfied). Co-ordination is about creating the *opportunity to perform*. Remember what we said about willingness, ability and opportunity? Opportunity, in the way the system is organized around people, accounts for as much as 90% of performance with the individual attributes of willingness and ability accounting for very much less. This is where coach and co-ordinate scores over command and control, because the latter tends to assume that focusing on the individual will make a big difference, when often they would do better if they simply weren't being held back.

By working on the system in which your people are working, you will help to create the conditions in which people can succeed. This is an important role because you are most likely to have access to the broader picture.

You can't expect the crew in Customer Servicing to know that the people in New Business are drowning in work since both Andrew and Ahmed went on paternity leave. That's where you come in. You liaise with other leaders to make sure that all of the business priorities are considered and then work with your team, or teams, to plan how to best cover all bases.

You can't expect Amanda to know if her genius new process improvement will work as well in Home Loans as it does in Collections. Again, you have a role in co-ordinating: working at the boundaries to make sure the complex and fluid organization keeps flowing and evolving positively.

And what do you do for the people in your team apart from act as the bridge to the rest of the operation? More directly, you support them through coaching.

Coaching is one of those modern management words that gets bandied about a lot to the point where it risks losing its meaning but it is an important word and is well chosen because it is quite different to teaching or training. Teaching tends to assume: I have the knowledge and you are ignorant. By the end of the teaching you will have some of my knowledge and be less ignorant. Training is more like: I have the skill and you don't. By the end of the training you will be able to do the job as well as me. In both cases, the relationship is dominated by the teacher or trainer. They are the one with the authority and the performer is a subordinate, passive recipient.

Coaching is entirely different. This is more like: you have the talent; I have the ability to bring out the talent in you. Think of it in the same way as coaching in sports: Béla Károlyi was the coach of the Romanian Olympic gymnastics team when Nadia Comăneci won gold and scored the first-ever perfect 10. There is no way this 34-year-old man could have done what she did, but he must have been able to create the environment in which the young gymnast was able to excel. With coaching, the emphasis is all on the performer. They *own* the performance and it is the coach's role to help them to reach their personal performance goals.

So, to summarize, your role as a Theory Y leader is to coach the individuals in your team to help them be the best versions of themselves and to work at the boundaries between your team (or department) and others so that the whole operation is co-ordinated.

What are you really for? Engaging and empowering

If you are a department manager or other senior manager with many people working for you organized into separate teams, we would say that a big part of your role is to push leadership and control as far away from you, and into your teams, as possible. You create the context that helps people to make the right decisions; you don't try to make all the decisions yourself. Leadership should be about engaging people to believe that they, and their roles, matter in the organization and empowering them to manage themselves as far as possible.

At the extreme, you could be supporting several 'self-managed' teams. There are many variations of this term 'self-managed'. You may well have heard of ideas such as self-directed teams, autonomous teams, leaderless teams or similar. You may even have pilots running for these in your own organization. From our perspective, these are nothing new. We can recall working on things like this in the early 1980s and there is literature from the 1960s on the same principles. It has come back into fashion recently with the concepts of Agile (more of this later if you are curious), so why is it that these ideas seem to wax and wane every couple of decades?

The idea keeps coming back because it is a good one. Decentralizing power and moving control as close to the customer as possible improves responsiveness and generates a greater sense of ownership and responsibility among workers delivering the service.

The idea keeps fading because it is rarely well implemented. Creating empowered teams represents a massive change to one part of the system, and remember what we have been saying about systems? Systems have a tendency to absorb and neutralize change (as all the elements of the system work to keep the status quo) or they tend to spiral out of control (like the cane toads) because one part of the system is so out of whack with the rest.

We will return to this subject in the final part of the book when we talk about new trends but suffice to say here that AOM supports devolved and decentralized management. We will tend to talk about 'team leaders' in subsequent chapters as a simple, if traditional, way to characterize a set of responsibilities. AOM will work equally well if the activities traditionally attached to a team leader are performed by a member of the team with special responsibilities for co-ordinating resources, or if the activities are shared or rotated around all team members.

A brief look at skills

There is a modern-day parable about the drunk man looking for his house keys underneath the streetlight outside his home. He probably dropped them a hundred yards up the road, but he figures: 'best to look here where I have got the light'. Sometimes the way people behave in their jobs can be governed in a similar way: not so much by the needs of the job but by what they are able to do.

If you have a manager in an insurance claims section who has come up through the ranks processing claims, they have a Masters in Insurance and Risk Management, and are a Fellow of the Chartered Insurance Institute, there is a strong chance that this will influence the way they manage their team. The focus is likely to be technical. Support may involve taking a difficult case off the team and doing it themselves. They might also be a brilliant people manager, but it is an oft-quoted lament that: 'We have promoted our best technician into becoming our worst manager.' Too harsh we are sure, but you see the idea: at some point, there is a cross-over in required skills from doing skills to managing skills. Traditionally, many people from team leader and up have had very strong technical skills but less emphasis has been placed on their people skills.

Of course, many operations have flipped this and gone down the route of saying the most important traits in their managers are the people skills because they are needed to motivate the team and they can always delegate the technical issues.

In the spirit of our core principle of *Actions Speak Louder Than Words*, what you train people in carries a very significant message about what you think is important. Training supports and underpins the behaviours that you want to see. Training managers in people skills tells everyone you see them as important. It shines the light in the right place.

If you are thinking about what training you should put on your own schedule, or on that of the managers who work for you, we recommend you think about three areas: technical, people and operational. Technical skills will be unique to your own operation. By people skills we mean the typical leadership skills of communicating, motivating and managing teams. But what about operational skills? We are talking here about the kind of skills that help to optimize performance. These include the ability to:

- prepare short, medium, and long-term plans that compare customer demand with resource supply;
- solve problems caused by imbalances between supply and demand, including effective prioritization of work, rescheduling of activities and redistributing resources;
- negotiate and trade resources with different groups within the operation with the abilities to both optimize own team performance and consider the wider operational perspective;
- monitor and control progress against plan so that as circumstances change, the optimal result can still be achieved;
- be open to both success and failure and to be able to review performance and learn lessons.

This is just a flavour of what we mean; you can contact us at ActiveOps for a fully worked Competence Profile for typical roles in operations if you want more detail.

Summary

- Changing performance means changing behaviour. Maybe you can't change the whole organization but your behaviours will influence all those who work for you, and very possibly influence the behaviours of others working around you (when you are particularly successful).

- Many organizations have cultures that could be described as reactive, bureaucratic or passive. These have related problems when it comes to delivering improved performance. At the very least, you can make your part of the operation active. You can be an active leader and you can encourage active management in the team leaders who work for you.

- AOM is like other forms of active management which are designed to optimize performance in complex systems. This involves using information to create feedback loops that will constantly seek to learn and improve.

- Choose wisely between Theory X, command and control and Theory Y, coach and co-ordinate. Match your style to the demands of the work and the abilities of the people you employ.

- Some organizations look to take the coach and co-ordinate policy to a level where teams become much more autonomous or self-directed. This is something we think can be very successful, but it will only work if people are given a framework, or a method, to work within.

- The behaviours you get will depend to some extent on the training you provide. People will nearly always play to their strengths.

In the next chapter we will start to spell out the AOM method.

Chapter 8
The AOM method and tools

The culture and behaviours that we talked about in the previous chapter were all about how *individuals* approach things; this chapter is about the *shared* activities of whole groups of people. This is what we mean when we talk about method: it is shared behaviour consciously designed and explicitly adopted. Technology plays a part here because the tools that you use make it easier for a group of people to all follow the same method.

Let's focus on method for now. If you want to change the culture or behaviours of a whole bunch of team leaders, you won't achieve it simply by exhortation. Try calling all your gang together and telling them: 'We're all going to be more Theory Y from now on.' You might get some funny looks but probably very little change. You can encourage the behaviours you want by focusing on the tangible things you can design and change.

If you set up mechanisms that make it easy for your team leaders to involve their teams in planning and target setting, or make it easy for them to help everyone to work together and collaborate, then you will change behaviours. This is what Richard Thaler and Cass Sunstein call a 'nudge' in their famous book, *Nudge: Improving Decisions About Health, Wealth, and Happiness*. An example of this is placing healthy foods more prominently at eyeline level in the school cafeteria. Doing this measurably increased the consumption of the healthy options.

The idea is to create circumstances that make it easier to do the 'right thing'. This might sound manipulative, but we would argue that it is just benign leadership. If you believe a certain way of working is good for your teams and your business, then making it easy to work that way just makes sense.

So what is the right thing to do in the world of service operations? What would a 'good' method look like in your world? The answer to these questions is embedded in the AOM method. We are going to describe that here and explain why it works so that you can build your own method.

There are two parts to this chapter.

- First, we will describe the management cycle at the heart of the method: *Forecast, Plan, Control, Review.* This is the routine sequence of events that happens every day, week and year.
- Next, we will talk about control in more detail. We don't mean command and control (which we suggested in the previous chapter is best in only limited circumstances); rather, we will show how you and your teams can stay in control of events instead of being buffeted around by uncertainties.

Remember, in this part of the book we are outlining the broad shape of what AOM is all about. Part 3 will go into lots more detail about how to actually design and implement the methods that we briefly describe here.

Will you have the authority to unilaterally make all the changes we are going to talk about? We obviously can't be sure about this but we are assuming that if you lead a group of people, and perhaps have a number of teams working for you, then almost certainly everything we are proposing could be done by you. Our experience in most organizations we have worked in suggests that the kind of things we are talking about are often done very differently from one department or one section to another, indicating that there is room for some individuality. So, go on, take the bull by the horns and see what changes you can make. Where you succeed will pave the way for others. You can be that pioneer!

The management cycle

You might have seen the trend for T-shirts or posters saying things like 'Eat, Play Golf, Sleep, Repeat' or 'Eat, Sleep, Rave, Repeat' (a song, we understand, by Fatboy Slim, Riva Starr and Beardyman). These slogans advertise people's particular obsession and suggest an endless cycle (of happiness we assume). Well, AOM has a cycle too, but there is no eating or sleeping involved.

AOM involves anticipating what work is coming down the tracks towards you and planning how you are going to get that work done (on time and to a good standard of quality). This is followed by actively controlling what you are doing from day to day to achieve that plan, and finally the cycle finishes with reviewing how well you did, learning any lessons… and repeat.

The AOM cycle looks like this:

Let's break this down into a bit more detail.

What matters to us in operations is the balance between work and time (having enough time to do the work and having enough work to fill the time) so we have put this at the centre of the picture. Around the outside is a loop: *Forecast, Plan, Control, Review*. Let's take each of these in turn.

Forecast

Forecasting is about expectation. The Met Office is forecasting rain; we think that we will get 10,000 new mortgage applications next month; we expect to lose 2% of our time to sick absence. Using historic data, market intelligence and whatever else you can get your hands on, a forecast gives you a starting point. Forecasts get you ahead of lead times. For example, it might take months to recruit and train new team members, so you need to know months in advance that your workload is going to increase sufficiently to require some new recruits. Forecasts are rarely perfectly accurate but it makes sense to have at least a rough direction of travel.

Plan

Where forecasting is about expectation, planning is about intention. I intend to take my brolly with me today because rain is forecast. (Other intentions were available: you could have decided to stay in bed for example.) In the work context, if you forecast high volumes of work coming in, you might plan to authorize overtime, or discourage annual leave, or borrow some resources from another team. The plan is your answer to how you intend to achieve your operational goals *given the forecast* of work to be done and resources available to do it.

Control

There is an old adage that no plan survives first contact with the enemy (apparently this was first said by the Prussian Field Marshal Helmuth von Moltke the Elder). Things change that weren't envisaged.

Control, then, is the activity of making the plan happen, or achieving the best possible outcome if variations to the forecast unfold. For example, if there is less work coming in than you forecast, can you find something else to keep your team fully occupied?

Review

This is about learning lessons so that we do better next time. How accurate was the forecast? How effectively did the plan deliver our performance requirements? How well did we control for the effects of going off plan? Reviewing and improving is, in our experience, the most overlooked part of the management cycle. It often seems to go: Forecast, Plan, Control, *Sleep*, Repeat. This is a loop of sorts but it cuts out the learning, the continuous improvement. As Einstein put it, 'The definition of insanity is doing the same thing over and over again, but expecting different results.' You have to learn and adapt.

Wheels within wheels

So how often will this cycle happen? This will depend to some extent on the nature of your operation and on the volume and variety of your work but typically we see team leaders (or the person representing an autonomous team if you are in a new, empowered, world) following this cycle on a weekly basis. They forecast and plan what they expect and intend to happen in each day of the coming week. Then as each day arrives, they do their best to stick to the plan and, at the end of the week, they learn lessons to improve their next weekly cycle.

If you are a department manager with a number of team leaders, you will probably be involved in co-ordinating the sharing of weekly plans but you may also be looking at a longer time horizon: monthly or quarterly. You might also report upwards to the wider operation on an even longer range: yearly or beyond.

This means that the F-P-C-R cycle is happening over different time horizons all of the time, a bit like a set of gears with one spinning very fast and turning the others more slowly.

What is the right time horizon? As we said about forecasting, this is linked to lead times, or how long it takes to make decisions happen. For example:

- If your decisions revolve around doing some work on Wednesday rather than Tuesday because Brian is on a course that day, your planning horizon is weekly.
- The same is probably true if you are looking to borrow Ashok for a day to cover for Brian.
- If you are looking to hire some people from the temp agency to cover a maternity leave, then you might be planning on a monthly or quarterly basis.
- If you are considering a large-scale reorganization with implementation of new robotics replacing ten jobs and creating some new high-skill customer service roles instead, then you are probably planning over a year or more.

All of these can be going on at the same time: wheels within wheels.

Controlling your destiny

We want to talk a bit more about the *Control* part of the cycle, conscious that earlier on we have rather put across the idea of 'control' as a dirty word. Indeed, in the context of command and control, in our view, the word is problematic. People generally don't need controlling; they need enabling. On the other hand, people do need to feel, and to be, *in control*.

Psychologists will tell you that *not being in control* is one of the most stressful conditions in the working environment. Feeling like you are just bobbing about like a cork in a stormy sea, buffeted by events, is not a great feeling. So when we talk about control in this context, we are talking about being in control: controlling events rather than being controlled by them.

It is also about controlling the things you can and accepting that some things will be beyond control. We have found that people working in unpredictable environments sometimes seem to give up on control because it just seems impossible. And yet, amidst all the uncertainty, a business might find that it is always busier at year end; Christmas comes round every year; most one-day absences happen on a Monday. In the midst of uncertainty, control the controllable and you will create more time and space to deal with the unpredictable.

Being in control might seem like an impossible dream for you right now. After all, if it were that easy everyone would already be doing it (and we wouldn't need to write about it). But it is not as hard as it might appear when you consider there are four ways of improving control:

- Employ the three key comparisons that help you use data to take control.
- Link control to time horizon (already mentioned above).
- Keep it visual. Control happens in the moment and this is easiest to achieve if people can see what is going on.
- Move control as close to the customer as possible.

The key comparisons – a brief excursion

There are three key comparisons that will help you to stay in control. These comparisons take raw and relatively unhelpful *data* and turn it into insightful and useful *information*. We will illustrate this by way of an example.

Daydream for a moment: Imagine you are sailing your Sun Odessy 440 yacht to the South of France (on a well-deserved break after successfully implementing AOM). You emerge from below deck, blinking into the sunlight after a brief siesta to ask your crew how things are going.

Brian happily informs you: 'We are heading due south, doing about 6 knots and the engine is running at about 3,000 rpm.'

Armed with these facts, you take it that the crew are still on top of everything and Saint-Tropez will hove into view very soon. You might as well go below and have another small gin and tonic…

But just as you turn to descend below deck back to your luxury cabin, Annie, says: '…or to put it another way, we are off course, we have been slowing down over the past two hours and the engine is in danger of overheating.'

With G&T now far from your thoughts, you look sternly at Brian and ask: 'Why didn't you say that?' He replies truculently: 'You didn't ask.'

It could be said that in response to your request for a status report, Brian did give you *accurate data*, but Annie gave you *useful information*. How do we lift information out of data? The answer is by using comparisons and this little story illustrates the three key comparisons of operations management: actual outcome compared to plan, actual outcome achieved over time and actual outcome compared to stands. Here they are in tabular form.

Data	Comparison	Data in context	Conclusion
We are going due south	Actual versus plan	We should be going south-east now	We are off course
We are doing about 6 knots	Actual over time	Two hours' ago we were doing 8 knots	We are slowing down
The engine is running at about 3,000 rpm	Actual versus standard	This engine should not run faster than 2,500 rpm	We are in danger of overheating the engine

Brian only gave you the first column. Annie cut out the middle two steps and gave you what you needed in the last column. It is these comparisons: against plan, over time and against standards that lift information out of mere data and, most importantly, make it *actionable*.

Okay, we're sorry to leave your daydream on a bleak note; feel free to return to it when you have a moment, and enjoy the Cote d'Azur, but for now just remember the three key comparisons. We will talk about these more when we discuss designing good reports and visual controls in Part 3.

Linking control to time horizons: How quickly should the wheels spin?

We mentioned earlier that the management cycle is actually a set of wheels within wheels and that the time horizon is linked to how quickly you need to respond. Another practical way to look at this is to consider what your own reporting deadlines are.

If you have to report that you hit 95% of telephone calls answered within 20 seconds for each day of the week, then you really need to have a feedback loop in place that works in real time or, at the very worst, hourly throughout the day.

If you have a weekly target to report on, then your control cycle can work on a daily basis. That way, if you know by Wednesday that you are drifting off plan, you still have time to do something about it. You get the idea.

Keep it visual: In sight, in mind not out of sight, out of mind

Remember, one of the core principles of AOM is 'keep plans in sight, in mind'. This idea of keeping things in sight is an important part of engaging the whole team and is also essential to good control. If people see that something is drifting off plan, they can do something about it. It is no good just reading about it in the end-of-period report.

In Part 3, we will describe specific types of charts and tables to put up on whiteboards for the whole team to see.

Getting close to the customer

What happens if you tread on a drawing pin in your bare feet? You don't think 'Hmm, I think I have trodden on something, I wonder what it is, perhaps I'd better move my foot before I do any damage...' No, you move your foot almost instantaneously (and maybe you scream and curse a bit). The thinking comes later.

Humans (in fact, most living creatures) are equipped with reflexes. Here, the reflex arc involves a receptor (that feels the pain) sending a signal to the spinal cord, which sends a signal back to a muscle (to make you jump away from the pain). There is no thinking involved: that can come later. Just respond in time for it to make a difference.

One can see the biological sense in being able to respond quickly and then think slowly. The same is true in operations. We would struggle if our brain were thinking: 'Okay now, breath in again... and out...' and we would struggle at work if central planning had to micro-manage every activity in a team. Imagine Central Planning calling down to the Claims Handling team and saying: 'Er, we've noticed that Wendy seems to be a little late back from her break. Probably on the phone continuing the row she had with her partner over breakfast. No biggie, but could someone pick up with Mr Jones, he is waiting on a response for arranging the respray of his car before he goes on his annual trip to Skegness?'

Don't get us wrong; there is a role for central planning (just as there is a role for a central nervous system) but sometimes you just have to be more responsive. Operations need to have their equivalent of a reflex nervous system where actions are taken in the moment and consequences and lessons come later. For that reason, we always recommend that you move operations control as close as possible to the customer. That is to say: control lies within a team – with the team leader or the people in the team.

A brief word on tools

We have built software specifically to support the method that we have outlined here. But we recognize that not everyone is going to be in a position to buy a top-end, enterprise-level planning technology so we have not made this book dependent on technology. Much of what we describe in Part 3 you can achieve with a whiteboard and a couple of spreadsheets. We can even help you get started if you get in touch with us via our website.

The key point about the tools that you use is that they make it easy for everyone to work in the same way. A nudge in the right direction. Tools also help methods to last from one generation of team leaders to the next. If everything relied on Active Annie, what would happen when she left or got promoted? All too often we have seen great processes in client operations that have been wholly dependent on one or two hero managers. By embedding method into tools (such as the way you draw up a daily planning whiteboard, or the way you organize a report of planned versus actual outcomes), you will encourage consistency, standardization and longevity.

Summary

The design principles we have set out in this chapter are based on two things. First and foremost, they represent our view of best practice in operations management. They also provide a nudge you can give to your teams to help them adopt the kinds of behaviours we talked about in Chapter 7.

Taken together, we believe that these behaviours (backed by the right skills) and methods (supported by the right tools) provide the best way of operating in complex human systems that we introduced in Chapters 5 and 6.

Management works best as a learning cycle involving the four stages of *Forecast, Plan, Control* and *Review*.

Control is key here: this is what puts the *A* in AOM. It is about being active rather than passive, or bureaucratic or reactive. Being in control requires you do the following:

- Use key comparisons to turn data into information: comparing actual outcomes to plan, to standard and different time periods.
- Make sure those comparisons happen in time to make a difference.
- Make comparisons visible so that everyone can engage and respond appropriately.
- Put control as close as possible to the customer so that you have great reflexes.

Okay, before we jump into Part 3 and start to build your own AOM framework, we will summarize Part 2 with a checklist. Chapter 9 offers you a cut-down version of the diagnostic framework we use when we are carrying out health checks for new clients.

Chapter 9
So how do you rate yourself?

How do you think you and your operation would rate against the AOM principles?

When we sit down and interview managers, team leaders and team members in the flesh, our diagnostic checklist goes into a lot of detail, but we have reproduced an overview of the main categories of our evaluation so that you can have a go for yourself. You will find out more about evaluating your current management systems, along with some client case studies, in your online toolkit at https://activeops.com/aomtoolkit.

The evaluation uses two of the frameworks that you have seen in this part:

- First, we evaluate everything against our simplified systems model that says that you have to make sure that Behaviour, Method, Skills and Tools are all consistent with each other and pulling in the same direction.
- Second, we evaluate your management method against our standard cycle of Forecast, Plan, Control, Review.

Contact us at ActiveOps if you would like to find out more about how you can do your own health check but for now have a think about the statements over the next few pages.

For each of the 16 statements, give yourself a score from 0 ('No, this doesn't sound like us') to 5 ('Yes, that is exactly what we are like').

Just to give you a sense of what we might find, a score of 30–35 is pretty common. Most organizations are good in parts but then have big gaps in other parts. Try to look for patterns in your own assessment:

- Are you particularly strong on certain aspects of the process (like forecasting) but could maybe do better in another area (such as reviewing)?
- Are your methods good, but the behaviours don't seem to match up? Or is it the other way around, and everyone is doing heroic work despite there being no standard method and with little help from the tools available?

As always, identifying strengths and weaknesses will help you to guide your actions.

In Part 3, we will put more flesh on the bone of the method, showing you how to build plans, balance work between teams, control performance to plan and learn lessons for next time.

But first have a look at the questions over the next few pages and assess your starting point.

The questionnaire

Forecasting

	Not at all	A little	Fifty/fifty	A lot	Always
Behaviour	Forecasts are realistic and not just compliant. Also, sensible levels of continuous improvement are built in. Forecasting is seen as a problem-solving process, not the start of a negotiation!				
Method	Activities exist for forecasting future volumes of work, and these forecasting activities engage the relevant people and incorporate any useful information, wherever they / it may be.				
Skills	Forecasting is not just the preserve of marketing or specialists, but day-to-day forecasting happens at the front-line.				
Tools	Workload forecasts use planning standards to convert work into time. This is further modified by using skill level or productivity to tune the forecast effort to the capability of the people involved.				

Planning

	Not at all	A little	Fifty/fifty	A lot	Always
Behaviour	People trust the plans they build and use them as part of serious conversations about business priorities, and then believe it is worth trying to 'make the plan happen'.				
Method	There is a clear structure of accountability and regular, routine meetings are held at the appropriate level to look at the relative workload in operating units. Processes for loaning and borrowing time (or moving work) between units are sensible and effective.				
Skills	All managers are able to build short and long-term plans, and effectively play their respective parts in planning meetings.				
Tools	Planning tools work on the same assumptions for work/time that longer-range forecasting tools do. The tools can aggregate and disaggregate plans.				

Controlling

	Not at all	A little	Fifty/fifty	A lot	Always
Behaviour	Managers constantly strive to deliver quality and service at the best cost. They understand and manage the relationships between these three drivers.				
Method	Managers communicate plans to staff and take regular corrective action to optimize performance. They meet regularly with their peers to deliver the best outcome for the whole enterprise - not just their part of the enterprise.				
Skills	Managers are able to interpret data correctly, so as to make the most effective decisions possible in the circumstances.				
Tools	Key operations reports are available in time to be useful. The data supports in-period control, and the capture of this seamlessly feeds both historical and present-time reporting.				

Reviewing

	Not at all	A little	Fifty/fifty	A lot	Always
Behaviour	Managers (at every level) treat data as an opportunity to learn lessons and improve. They focus on the facts, rather than on blaming others and/or looking for excuses.				
Method	There are regular and timely meetings in place to review performance against plan, so as to learn lessons for future planning. These happen from front-line to boardroom.				
Skills	Managers are able to address individual performance issues - they have both personal skills and knowledge of the organization's procedures. They are also able to drive continuous improvement through projects, problem solving, process analysis.				
Tools	The tool set supports the review process, and is flexible in easily incorporating lessons learned - for example, increasing productivity, changes in planning standards, new work types, new staff etc.				

How did you do? Don't worry if you haven't scored very high, and equally we recommend that there may still be room for improvement if you have given yourself top marks. It will be worth looking back at this after you have read through Part 3 to see if you want to adjust any of your scores.

Part 3

The AOM method in action

In this part we will give you what you need to make a practical start doing AOM in your own business.

Chapter 10 gives you an overview including a process map which acts as the wiring diagram for the whole method.

Chapter 11 introduces some of the basic ideas and terminology used in AOM so that we can ensure we are all talking the same language.

Chapters 12 to 16 walk you through the whole management cycle from building a weekly operating plan, through managing events to deliver the best possible outcome and on to reviewing performance to learn lessons and improve for next time.

Chapter 10
Overview of the AOM method

The Colt 45 Peacemaker

In the very early days of implementing the AOM method with clients, we were invited to carry out some work with a large UK public-sector operation. The leaders of this operation were very respectful of the collective representation in place, and we were asked to present our plans to the trade unions before the work got underway.

Neil was very happy to do this. He had worked with trade unions on several occasions and was confident that our message was a very positive one about supporting staff and making sure they would be treated fairly. He hoped that this would be well received and this was indeed the case in the first couple of presentations to local trade union groups, with one even saying that AOM should have been implemented a long time ago.

But then one particular meeting took a very different turn. The senior union representative and his team listened politely to everything he had to say, asked a couple of clarifying questions and then turned to their manager and said: 'If this man comes on site here, we will walk off site.'

What followed was a difficult discussion in which Neil could play no part as various historic grievances were aired. Neil was somewhat crestfallen that his passion for believing in and championing front-line workers had not come across and he felt a bit awkward as, on the way out of the meeting, he ended up by chance travelling down the lift with the senior representative. The rep turned to Neil and said rather cryptically: 'Please don't take this personally. It is just that you came into the meeting with a Colt 45 and called it a Peacemaker but our worry is that it will be used to shoot us.'

On the way home on the train, Neil reflected on what the union man had said. Was he arming management with a tool to victimize staff as the union representative had suggested? He could understand the rep's point of view. Although Neil's intentions for the method were all completely positive, that could not stop others using the same activities that we will describe in this part of the book in very different ways.

We did not share the union's distrust of the management and happily we were largely proved right. In the end, the project did go ahead and the trade unions were broadly co-operative once their concerns had been mostly addressed. The project was a success and staff and management both felt they benefitted.

We mention this cautionary tale here because this part of the book is going to focus on elements of the method in some detail. You might worry about how these methods could be used and how your people might react to them. If so, look back into Part 2 to understand the intention behind the actions. That way we are sure you will make them work for you in a positive and constructive way.

***

This part of the book is going to tell you how to implement AOM, and will do it in quite a lot of detail. What you learn in this part will equip you to be able to build the bones of a planning and control system for your own part of your operation.

To give you an overview of this, we are going to present you with a flow chart. Process maps and flow charts are all the rage these days, either for analysing a business process to cut out waste, or to automate parts of it, or simply just to document the standard operating procedure. It seems odd to us that there is rarely the same attention paid to the standard operating procedure for the *management process*. This process is the one that sits above, and has an influence on, all the other processes that go on in your teams so this one should be your number one priority. Shaving a few minutes out of one process or automating most of another will deliver a fraction of the benefit that could be achieved by having a clear, effective and shared process adopted by everyone responsible for managing work in your teams. So, with that in mind, we will present the *Management Process Flow*.

In the last chapter of Part 2, we said that the management process was a loop:

We also said that this could be a loop of loops as it could operate over different time horizons. So, we are going to build weekly plans based on weekly forecasts, monthly plans based on monthly forecasts and so on. We are also going to control how we perform towards achieving our weekly plan by reviewing it daily. Our monthly plan we will review weekly. Eat, sleep, plan, repeat.

The flow chart we are building up to is all about activities and *meetings*. Activities such as planning or controlling are linked to certain key meetings.

- *Loading meetings* are where plans are shared and discussed between teams to make sure work and resources are shared effectively.
- *Commitment meetings* are where plans are shared and discussed within teams so that everyone is committed to the same outcome.
- *Variance meetings* are where outcomes are compared to the plan and lessons learned so that the process can continue to improve.

In the following diagram, we have depicted activities as boxes and meetings as clouds. We have also put in a few icons to suggest where some *visual controls* (charts and tables) might be looked at.

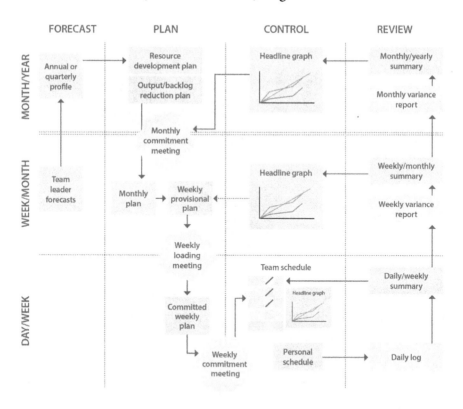

The best way to understand this is to take a week in the life of Active Annie and her team of all-star claims advisors. We will take the flow chart in bite-sized chunks.

A week in the life of Active Annie.
Thursday 7 November

We join Annie on an unsea-
sonably wet Thursday in
November as she thinks
about what will face her
Motor Claims team next
week.

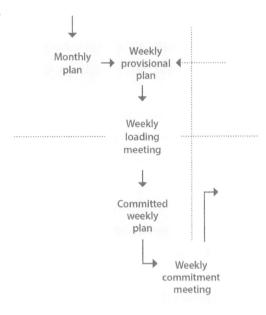

- By way of context,
  Annie has in front
  of her the *Monthly
  Plan* for November
  that she confirmed
  a couple of weeks
  ago. This includes
  certain   expecta-
  tions for the volumes of work to be done, but crucially she also
  has a plot of known holidays, a training course and a commitment to give some time to the RPA analysts. (Yes, the robots
  are coming.)
- Annie now turns her attention to the coming week and starts
  to prepare her *Weekly Provisional Plan*. She first looks at her
  forecast data. It has been raining a lot and motor claims are
  up on last year. She tweaks her volume forecast up a couple of
  per cent based on what she has learned over the past couple of
  weeks. (That's Annie using the feedback loop – learning from
  the recent past.)
- With the forecast updated, Annie starts to plan how much work
  needs to get done. With the high workload and a couple of
  other issues in the past weeks, she has some backlogs of work.
  To get back in line with her target service levels, Annie needs to

plan to do more than just keep pace with the forecast workload. She plans to eat into the backlog as well.

- Okay, Annie is getting a bit worried now. That looks like a lot of work. Will Xian and Yousuf still get to do their GDPR training or will she have to cancel it? She leaves it in the plan for now and looks at who is likely to be in next week.

- With no known sick leave and no one on holiday, Annie has pretty much a full team but when she looks at how much time the team has available compared to the amount of work needed to be done to get back on target, she is nearly 15 hours' short of what she needs for the week.

- What to do? Cancel the GDPR training? That would help a bit but it is important and cancelling it would send the wrong signal. Work overtime? Annie is empowered to authorize it but doesn't want to spend if she doesn't have to. Leave the backlogs for another week? Not exactly customer first is it?

- Annie waits. Her *Provisional Plan* is 15 hours' short but she takes this along to the *Loading Meeting*. We will assume that you are chairing this and you hold the ring as Annie and the other team leaders share their plans. As it turns out, Reactive Ronnie's New Business team is bang up to date. (Ronnie might look like the hero here but it was just a fluke; he's still not the best at planning and control.) Ronnie can lend Annie the 15 hours she needs. He'll actually lend 20 hours. He does have some people who worked in claims in the past but they may be a little slow now because they are a bit rusty at claims, having moved out of that section a while ago.

- Annie walks out of the *Loading Meeting* quite happy. She can stick with her plan, get the training done and get the back logs under control. She quickly updates her plan which is now what she will call her *Committed Plan* for next week.

A week in the life of Active Annie.
Friday 8 November

- Annie comes to work on the Friday with a spring in her step, despite the driving rain. She has a plan that she knows will work. The team get together for their daily huddle. The Friday huddle is always a bit different because it is their *Commitment Meeting*. This is where they look at the plan for next week and all agree that they can get it done.

- Remember, we are portraying Annie as a fairly traditional team leader. She is doing the planning and representing her team at the loading meeting but this need not be such a traditional, hierarchical role. Annie could, in your organization, be the team member who specializes in liaising with other teams, or the team member whose turn it is to take a planning lead. All organization configurations are catered for – because the activities remain the same. Now, back to Annie and the team.

- Annie says to the team she knows it has been a bit tough and no one likes the work piling up but, with a bit of assistance from Ronnie's team, it should be possible to get back on track and also to keep the training commitments in place. She asks if some of the work queues could be diverted to give the loanees from Ronnie's team some work for the early part of next week.

- Annie reflects on the process here. What a good idea it is to plan for next week on a Thursday. This gives us time to set up any work or staff movements and it gives us a positive focus to our Friday meeting.

A week in the life of Active Annie.
Monday 11 November

We re-join Annie after a quiet, but still wet weekend…

- Annie sets up her whiteboards with the anticipated plans for the week and for Monday in particular.

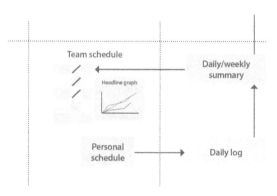

- At the morning huddle, everyone agrees what part they are going to play that day, but the best-laid plans of Friday have already gone slightly awry as one of the people being loaned from Ronnie's team has not turned up.
- The team agree what they can get done and what a good outcome for the day would look like.

A week in the life of Active Annie.
Tuesday 12 November

- We now see the beginnings of the first feedback loop.
- Annie reviews the data captured on Monday on how much work came in and how much was done. She updates the whiteboards and the charts that give everyone a clear idea of how they did yesterday.
- The plans are updated in the light of yesterday's outcomes and off we go again. Everyone is clear and committed.
- Not for the first time, Annie reflects after the meeting how easy it is to maintain a positive sense of urgency and to avoid a sense of crisis. Everyone knows what they need to do for the team, no one is being asked (implicitly or explicitly) to achieve the

impossible and so everyone feels committed and positive about their contribution.

A week in the life of Active Annie.
The rest of the week (and beyond)

The week continues with this daily feedback loop so that the team stays as close as it can to the plan but making sensible judgements to shift priorities to do the best they can as circumstances unfold. They have to respond to a continuing increase in claims and dial back on some of their internal development activities. They also don't get the backlogs down to quite where they wanted, but at least everyone knows that they did the best they could with the situation they faced.

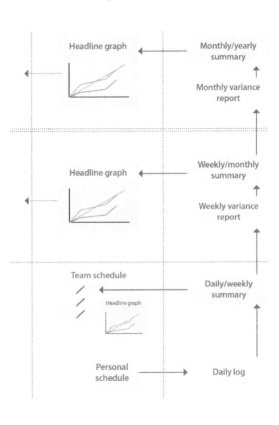

- As Annie uses the daily data to work with her team and help them to have their best week possible, the same data is also compiled and collated to provide feedback on longer-range plans – both monthly and yearly. This is no trouble to Annie because the data has already been captured and used, but it is now feeding into the data that is flowing up to you as department manager.

So we leave Annie and her team coping with the extra claims for bumps and scrapes that have come with the heavy rain. We can see that she has been working with her team on a simple control loop, constantly using data from who has done what work to compare progress against plan and then to plan what next.

How does her team feel about all this data being collected on what work they have done? Does it feel like they are being watched by the proverbial Big Brother? No, it doesn't. The key thing is that there is a massive difference between collecting data *on people* or collecting data *for people*. Annie is doing the latter. She is collecting the data to help them to plan the next day, so that collectively they have a successful day, every day and every week. She isn't collecting data to judge people, to shame them or to reward them.

The good news beyond this is that the data collected to support the local planning and control process can then also flow up to you, the department manager, so that you can see how things are going on a longer timeframe. You can also aggregate Annie's data along with Brian's, Percy's and Ronnie's to get a picture of your whole department. Crucially, the data you are getting not only tells you how your teams are performing; it also tells you how in control they are. You are seeing all those key comparisons: against plan, against standards and over time. You are not trying to drive by looking into the rear-view mirror that is historical reporting; you are looking at reports that tell you whether you can stay relaxed (with your feet up on the desk if you like) because everything is under control, or if you need to get out and support one or more of your teams if things are starting to slip.

Like your team leaders, you are maximizing performance, not by beating up individuals or getting them to work to the beat of a drum, not by doing Theory X management, but by managing the system that supports and enables people to perform. You design and maintain the management cycle and let the people get on with serving the customers.

The remaining chapters in Part 3 will go into a lot more detail on how to produce a plan like Annie's, how to run a loading meeting to balance plans between different teams, how to control from day to day and how to review lessons learned and go again. First, we want to make sure we are all talking the same language. We know that jargon can be a pain in the neck, but words and their meanings are important. If you and a colleague have different definitions of productivity, it can be hard to pull together for the greater good. This is the subject of the next chapter.

Chapter 11

Back to basics

No, we are not referring to the ill-fated campaign launched by Prime Minister John Major in 1993 intended to be a return to traditional values. If you are too young to remember this or have wiped it from your mind, it wasn't a great success. Nor, indeed, are we talking about Christina Aguilera's fifth studio album, *Back to Basics*, which includes the track 'Candyman', a tribute of sorts to the war-time music of the Andrews Sisters. When we say back to basics, we are talking about basic thinking, principles and calculations that are at the heart of all operations management.

Don't worry if you thought that the best use for a maths lesson at school was to finish your English homework. We promise to be gentle with you.

The ideas of standard times, utilization and productivity are pretty common, hence us saying back to basics, but we briefly discuss these here so that you can see how these are used 'the AOM way'. This will help you to make the best of AOM and to compare and contrast the AOM method with anything currently in place in your operation, or anything that has been proposed to you by others.

Common currency

We're going to dive right in with a discussion about standard times. This is an idea which can be both controversial and confusing. But it is actually very simple, straightforward and just what you need at the heart of your planning systems.

Let's start with a simple analogy. Before heading off on a trip to Kruger National Park, you rummage about in your bottle full of small change to see what currency you have. You find the following:

- Five English one pound coins
- Ten one euro coins
- Three US dollar coins.

So, how much money do you have? Although the answer: 'I have 18 coins' would be true, it would also be pretty meaningless. It would make much more sense to say what the coins are worth. You could convert their values into any one of the above currencies, but since you are off to South Africa, let's see what you have if we convert all of the above into rand.

At the time of writing, you would get something like the following:

Coins		Conversion rate	Rand
5	Pounds	19.12	95.60
10	Euros	16.36	163.60
3	Dollars	14.77	44.31
		Total	303.51

So, 18 coins but also a little over 300 rand. Okay, that might not be quite enough to buy you and your travelling partner a meal when you step off the plane, but at least you have a meaningful estimate of the value of your coins.

Putting this into a work context, imagine that Hema and Anoop work for a rather old-fashioned boss who wants to evaluate his employees' performance. He has not had a good week and is itching to take it out on someone. (Clearly not very 'AOM' this boss, we'll have to work on him, but this will show why it is so important to ensure work is measured in a fair and transparent way.) The Bad Boss looks at the following chart and broods over which of his two employees has done the most work…

	Work done	
	Hema	Anoop
Review written applications	20	80
Answer phone calls	80	-
Respond to emails	50	10

As with the coins, it doesn't make a lot of sense to just look at 'bits of work'. What if Bad Boss were to say to Anoop: 'How come you have only done 90 when Hema has managed 150? See me in my office…'?

We might have a gut feeling that Anoop is being hard done by (Anoop certainly thinks so!) but what evidence do we have? We need to do what we did with the coins so that we can total the amount of work done by each person in a 'common currency' of some sort.

But what should we pick as our standard currency? Rand again? Potentially we could convert everything into rand but how do you put a value on answering a phone call? The usual answer in a circumstance like this is to convert all the units of work into the amount of time that it would typically take to do the work. This is often called a *standard time*.

Let us say that the standard time for reviewing written applications is 20 minutes. That is to say that *on average* it takes a properly trained person about 20 minutes to review one application. Hema has done 20 of these, so the amount of work we have is 20 times 20 minutes. That is 400 minutes or 6.66 hours' worth of work.

If we apply standard times to all three tasks for both people, we can then add up the amount of work that they have done. Thus:

	Standard time (mins)	Work done		Work at standard (hours)	
		Hema	Anoop	Hema	Anoop
Review written applications	20	20	80	6.67	26.67
Answer phone calls	5	80	-	6.67	0.00
Respond to emails	10	50	10	8.33	1.67
			Totals	21.67	28.33

So Hema has done nearly 22 hours' worth of work in the week, while Anoop has done just over 28 hours' worth of work. Despite doing more items of work, Hema has done less work when it is all converted into the same currency.

Notice we have said 'hours' worth' of work. We are not saying Hema has spent 22 hours working on these tasks. No one has been following her round with a stopwatch. No, we have simply converted the different amounts of work that she and Anoop have done into a standard measurement based on the typical time to complete the tasks.

We said at the start of this part that standard time can cause confusion and controversy. Why? First confusion: as we have just pointed out, 22 hours of standard time is an amount of work; it might have taken more or less actual time to do that work. Yes, that can be a little confusing.

And controversial? Timing work does have quite a controversial past: for some, it conjures up images of people with clipboards and stopwatches following people around. People imagine that the standard time is the time you *must* take to do a job, and you have to work slavishly to the beat of the drum. This is not what we mean by standard times, but we know that some people have long memories. To be clear:

standard times are just a way to convert various items of work into the common currency of time (just as we used rand and a common currency earlier).

Converting everything into standard time makes it possible for us to add up diverse types of work, which not only makes reporting easier (and fairer) but also makes forward planning possible. For a given mix of work, we can estimate how much time we should allow to complete it. But before we get to that sort of forward planning, there is one more thing we need to explore. Although we know that Anoop did more hours' worth of work, we haven't yet considered how much time it *actually* took him to do it. What if poor old Anoop only did six hours' more work than Hema by staying late every night working extra hours? Maybe in fact he ended up working twice as many hours as Hema?

Without this information we could make false assumptions, such as assuming Anoop can get more work done and then giving him extra when he is already getting home too late to put his kids to bed. So far, we know the amount of work that both have done but we don't yet know how much time it took to complete. Comparing the standard hours of work done to the number of actual hours used to do the work is essential both to report people's achievements fairly and for planning ahead accurately.

This is measurement of work done in time available is called *productivity*.

Productivity

Productivity is simply a measure of how much time it took to complete a certain amount of work. Let's have a look at the breakdown of Hema and Anoop's working week. We start with the pair's base working hours of 35 hours a week and then find out how much time they actually spent doing the work by subtracting the time spent elsewhere. By convention, we think about 'downtime' being time lost to the business such as through sickness or holiday. If someone was in the office but doing things other than working on the 'core work', we call that 'diverted time'. Diverted time includes things like training, going to meetings, having a one-to-one with a supervisor. (You can make up your own categories, but splitting lost and diverted time makes sense, as you will see later when we talk about planning.) Here, then, are the figures for Hema and Anoop.

	Hema	Anoop
Base Working Hours	35	35
Downtime		
Holiday	7	
Sickness		
Diverted Activity		
Training	2	
Meetings	1	1
One-to-one		
Core Hours	25	34

Hema works a 35-hour week but had a day's holiday on Monday. She also had two hours' training and went to an hour-long meeting in the week. As a result, she had 25 hours available to spend 'on the day job'.

Note: we haven't followed Anoop to the toilets and haven't timed how much time Hema talked with colleagues about last night's hockey match. There is often a feeling that looking at how people spend time will be intrusive, and of course it could be. It won't be if you only focus on the level of detail that matters. By starting with base working hours and then only taking away the 'big-ticket items' like training or being on holiday, all the day-to-day little things are left in as part of the natural working day. Sure, some days your staff might chat more than others or even take longer in the loo. But anyone worrying about that sort of detail really needs to get out more. Remember, the reason we want some data on how people have spent their time is to make sure that we can fairly reflect on how much effort was truly required to achieve an amount of work. Not to spy on people or question how they spend their time.

So it took Hema 25 hours to do the 150 bits of work that she did that week, or 21.67 hours' worth of work (based on our standard times from above). This gives us the following calculation for Hema's productivity.

$$\text{Hema's productivity} = \frac{\text{Work Done}}{\text{Time Worked}} = \frac{21.67}{25} = 87\%$$

And in the same way:

$$\text{Anoop's productivity} = \frac{\text{Work Done}}{\text{Time Worked}} = \frac{28.33}{34} = 83\%$$

Hema's productivity is just slightly higher than Anoop's.
Okay, still with us? What do we know now?

- Hema did more 'bits of work' than Anoop, but that was misleading.
- If we look at that in terms of a common currency (based on standard times), Anoop did more work than Hema. But this still doesn't tell the whole story.
- Hema did do less work than Anoop but she also worked fewer hours than him. In fact, Hema's productivity is slightly higher than Anoop's. That is to say that she got more work done in the time she had available than he did in the time he had available.

Utilization

Before moving on, we want to introduce one more definition, and that is *utilization*. As the term suggests, this is some measure of how much something was used. Looking back at Hema's week:

- She works a 35-hour week but was on in the office for 28 hours because she had a one-day holiday.
- Of those 28 hours in the office, two were spent in meetings and she had a one-hour one-to-one session, leaving 25 hours to be spent on the core work.

You could say she used 25 hours to do the work that she did. So her utilization of the time she spent in the office can be calculated thus:

$$\text{Utilization (of Attended Time)} = \frac{\text{Time used on Core Work}}{\text{Time in Attendance}} = \frac{25}{28} = 89\%$$

Utilization is a useful measure because:

- if it is too low it suggests that your people are always off training or in meetings (adhering to that old maxim: 'never let work get in the way of a good meeting');
- if it is too high then people are never being given any support or training.

What is too high or too low? You will have to judge this for yourself depending on the nature of your work, your people and your overall approach to things. We can't dictate on this one.

In summary:

- Standard times are used to measure an amount of work in a fair and repeatable way. This way work of very different kinds can all be added together.

- Productivity is a measure of how much effort was put in to achieve a certain level of output.
- Utilization is a measure of how much of the time spent in the office was spent doing the core work.

Questions and objections

If you are not used to this way of thinking about work and time, you may well have some questions, and if you were to implement this to a number of teams you would definitely get a few. Trust us, we've done it hundreds of times and get a lot of very similar questions. Most of these questions reflect genuine concerns that should be addressed. AOM is a fair and honest way of trying to help teams to be the best they can be and if it doesn't feel like that then we must take the time to address everyone's concerns.

Here are some of the common issues that arise.

1. Are you saying I should take 20 minutes to answer every letter?

   No, absolutely not! Sometimes companies call these standard times other things like 'should take times' or 'reasonable expectations (REs)'. In our view that is a mistake. For each individual on any given task, they should take as long as is necessary to do the job right for the customer. The standard time is simply an average that we use as a conversion factor so we can add up all sorts of different types of work together. Averages, by their nature, will mean that some tasks take more time and some less. Don't try to work to the average; just do the work. This is not about dictating the pace people should work at like galley slaves rowing to the beat of the drum.

2. So if I finish the task in 18 minutes, can I have two minutes' break?

(Yes, we really have been asked that!). I refer my learned friend to the answer above… Don't focus on the times; focus on the customers.

3. And should I hang up if the call goes over five minutes?

   Big patient sigh… see above. Don't focus on the time; focus on the customer!

4. According to this report, I only did five hours of work yesterday. That can't be right; I was here all day: no meetings, no interruptions. Literally at my desk all day. Your sums must be wrong.

   Remember, no one is saying that you only worked for five hours. Saying you did five standard hours (or five hours' worth) of work is a measure of the *amount* of work done, not the time taken. There could be all sorts of reasons why you only did five hours' worth of work in an eight-hour day. Maybe you were unlucky and, for a lot of your tasks, it took longer than average for you to delight the customer. Maybe some of the work was stuff that you are not so experienced at and no one was expecting you to work at the average pace of others. Maybe we have got the averages wrong and they need adjusting.

5. I have just come out with 110% productivity for the week. That can't be right can it?

   It might seem logical to say that you can't be more than 100% productive but remember what we are doing here: we are measuring how many standard hours of work you did in the time you had available. It would be possible for you to work for six hours but manage to do seven hours' worth of work and get a productivity of over 110%. This could happen if some of the tasks you were doing were easier than the average so you got through more of them. It could also be that if you are more skilled than average, then you might always do better than 110%. Remember: the standard times are set at an average, not a maximum, so it must be possible for some people to go over 100% productivity. By the same token, it is perfectly reasonable and acceptable that some people will have productivity below 100%. That's averages for you.

6. So, do I get marked down in some way if my productivity is low?

No, that is not what this is about. Measuring productivity is our way of making sure that our conversion of work into standard time is representative of all people. It helps us to make sure that our standard times are right and the assumptions we are making are reasonable. Productivity is about measuring our planning process, not about measuring people. That said, if you consistently score lower on productivity than most other people in your team, you might want to consider what this is telling you and if there are things you could do to improve.

Chapter 12
Your first plan

In this chapter, we will outline how to produce a plan for the coming week. Our example is simplified but not simplistic. It should give you all you need to prepare a plan in your own area, or to coach your team leaders to prepare plans for you. You will also be able to find some helpful tools and guides in your online tool kit at https://activeops.com/aomtoolkit.

Remember: planning is at the heart of good operations management. Looking at reports and data is always like driving by looking in the rear-view mirror. It is an emphasis on looking back that leads to management cultures of reward and punishment, blame and recrimination. Planning is what creates involvement and engagement; it is what creates opportunity to perform and what separates great teams and great organizations from merely good ones. (Yep, you may have noticed, we really like planning.)

The planning balance sheet

We can think of the planning process a bit like a balance sheet with work on one side and resources on the other, thus:

Work	Resources
Core Work	Staff Complement
Task 1	*less*
Task 2	Holidays
Etc	Sickness

On the work side, we have *Core Work*. These are the main tasks that account for the bulk of a team's work. It is these that we measure using standard time so that they can be represented in a common currency, as we discussed in the previous chapter. The resources side starts with the *Staff Complement* (the base working hours of the whole team) and then subtracts time lost to things like holidays and sickness.

So far, so good, but which side of the balance sheet should we put things like training, meetings and so on? They could go on the right-hand side and be subtracted from the time available to do the core work, or they could go on the left and be added onto the work to be done.

Mathematically, it makes little difference but in terms of the message and values we want to portray, there is a big difference. We want to demonstrate that training, meetings and suchlike are positive things to plan to achieve, not negative things taking time away from doing work. Have you ever had a situation where something important like training or performance meetings have been cancelled due to work pressures? What signal does this send? It is for these reasons that we don't like to put training and suchlike on the same side as sickness or holidays.

We call things that are done in the office but are not core work *Diverted Activity* because, although important, they are diverting time away from the customer. When we are planning, we add these on to the 'work' side of the balance sheet because they are important activities and we should try to find the time to do them. (Remember one of the core principles of AOM: Keep things in sight, in mind.)

And so the balance sheet now looks like this:

Work	Resources
Core Work	Staff Complement
Task 1	*less*
Task 2	Holidays
Etc	Sickness
Diverted Activity	
Activity 1	
Activity 2	

To finish this off, we need to calculate whether or not we have enough time (or too much) to do the work. So we need a balance figure and then need to consider what actions we might take if our plan is not balanced.

The full balance sheet will look like this:

Work	Resources
Core Work	Staff Complement
Task 1	*less*
Task 2	Holidays
Etc	Sickness
Diverted Activity	**Balance**
Activity 1	**Actions**
Activity 2	Flexitime
	Overtime
	Borrow
	Loan

Let's look at this by way of an example.

Continuing from where we got to with Anoop and Hema in the last chapter, and the three tasks that they had to work on, let's imagine that they are part of a team of ten people, all doing this work. We are going to set up a scenario and then walk you through producing a plan.

The work side of the balance sheet

1. Review written applications.

    We expect an average of 50 applications a day or 250 for the week. We have a bit of a backlog of these at the moment so want to clear out more than we are expecting to come in. We aim to clear 300 applications next week. Processing 300 applications at 20 minutes a go is 6,000 minutes of work, or 100 hours.

2. Phone calls.

    This isn't a contact centre but all our agents will take and deal with phone calls as part of their work. (Dedicated contact centre planning is a big subject we are going to miss out here while we keep things simple.) We expect about 160 calls a day or 800 over the course of the week.

3. Emails.

    Customer expectation of emails is that they get a pretty quick response so we aim to answer all emails on the day of receipt. We expect to get 500 in during the course of the week and so want to plan to answer 500.

This gives us the first part of our plan.

Core Work	Standard	Target	Hours
Applications	20	300	100
Phone calls	5	800	67
Emails	10	500	83
Hours required at standard			250

So, we have to budget to have time to do 250 hours of work.

Not so fast!

What if Anoop and Hema had been running the team's lottery syndicate and their numbers came up a few weeks ago? You might have a whole bunch of new recruits in the team and it would be very unlikely that they would be able to work at the pace suggested by the standard times. (Remember, they were based on work of average difficulty being done by an average, well-trained person.)

Under these circumstances, you might want to assume that the team's productivity would only be 50%. That is to say, it would take them twice as long to do the work than the standards would suggest. So not 250 hours but 500 hours.

Luckily for us (but not for Hema and Anoop et al), they didn't win the lottery; they are still plugging away with their lucky numbers but still doing the day job. Now, we still need to be realistic about what the team can achieve so we don't just take the standard times at face value. If we look back over the past few weeks, we find the following weekly productivity scores.

Week	1	2	3	4	5
Productivity	75%	70%	75%	77%	90%

What level of productivity should we plan for? We could say 90%; after all, they achieved that last week. But no, the team leader thinks that would be a bit of a stretch – it looks like a one-off compared to the other figures. On the other hand, 70% looks a bit low and there has been a rising trend over the past few weeks. Let's go for 80% productivity. (There is more science behind this, which we will come back to, but common sense is nearly always as good, if not better than science anyway.) In fully engaged and empowered teams, this number will be arrived at by working with the team, not imposing it upon them. There is no point in setting this at a value no one thinks they could achieve.

So, recent history tells us that Anoop, Hema and the team, on average, take longer than the standard times when doing their work. To be realistic about what can be done, we should allow for this in our plan. Using 80% productivity for our plan means the team is likely to need 313 hours to get done the 250 hours of work available. (Remember: Productivity = Work Done/Time Worked. So, 250/313 = 80%.)

Now, building our anticipated productivity into our plan gives us the following:

Core Work	Standard	Target	Hours
Applications	20	300	100
Phone calls	5	800	67
Emails	10	500	83
Hours required at standard			250
Productivity	80%		
Total hours required			313

You will see that the total hours required to do the work has gone up from 250 to 313 to allow for the team working at 80% of the standard rate. This is therefore the amount of time that we want to set aside next week for the team to serve the customers – without rushing, to a high, professional standard.

Now we add in the diverted activity.

Core Work	Standard	Target	Hours
Applications	20	300	100
Phone calls	5	800	67
Emails	10	500	83
Hours required at standard			250
Productivity	80%		
Total hours required			313

Diverted Activity	Standard	Target	Hours
Training			14
One-to-one			3
Total hours required			330

Here we have added in two days (14 hours) of training and three hours of one-to-one coaching, bringing the total hours we need to find for next week up to 330.

The time side of the balance sheet

So now let's complete the balance sheet and see what we have if we compare the work to be done with the time available to do it.

WORK				TIME	
Core Work	Standard	Target	Hours	Resources	
Applications	20	300	100	Staff Complement	350
Phone calls	5	800	67	Downtime	
Emails	10	500	83	Sickness	0
Hours required at standard			250	Holiday	35
Productivity	80%				
Total hours required			313	Total hours available	315
Diverted Activity	Standard	Target	Hours	Actions	
Training			14	Flexitime	
One-to-one			3	Overtime	
				Borrow	
Total hours required			330	Loan	

You can see that we started with ten full-time employees working a 35-hour week (that's 350 hours); we then lost 35 hours because someone has booked a week's holiday. There is no known sick absence. The net effect is to have 315 hours available to do 330 hours of work. We are 15 hours' short of what we need.

Quite often, the first time we do a plan such as this with a new team, the reaction is something like: 'Well, that just confirms what we've known for a long time. We can't get everything done.' The implication is that the plan should now be put on one side and everyone should just do the best they can. That's passive management, not active. What would happen if nothing gets done to address that shortfall of 15 hours? Maybe:

- the training will get cancelled;
- we don't reduce the backlog in applications as much as intended;
- we get lucky and not so many phone calls and emails come in;
- everyone just works that bit harder, maybe cutting a few corners to get through.

The point is *something will happen* and the only question is: will it be something that happens to you or something that is made to happen by you? The point of Active Operations Management is about taking control of events, not being dictated to by them.

We will come back to look at ways of balancing a plan in much more detail later but our key message is that the plan gives the team and team leader the power to decide.

A nice problem to have?

What if the plan had worked out slightly differently and there had been surplus time rather than a shortage? While this might seem like not much of a problem, the same argument applies: having surplus hours in not necessarily a problem, but it should be a call to action. Are you going to let something happen, or make something happen?

The results of passive management could be:

- the team slows down so that the right amount of work gets done but it just takes more time;
- we eat into the applications backlog and get ahead of our service-level targets.

The problem with the first of these is that productivity will be lower and the cost of completing the work higher than the team is capable of achieving. This kind of accidental under-performance is what we were talking about when we described latent capacity in Chapter 3 and how many operations are able to achieve more than they appear able to because they let these opportunities slip through their fingers.

The second possibility: of getting ahead on applications processing, and maybe even improving on customer service, seems like less of a problem. Indeed, viewing one team in a silo, it may well be that the best thing to do with some surplus time is to get ahead of the game. But teams rarely exist in complete isolation. What if the Premium Servicing team is struggling to keep up with customer renewals because they have had a recent period of absenteeism and are falling behind? Maybe if Hema and Anoop's team had some surplus time it would be better if they helped out Premium Servicing rather than just get ahead of their own targets. We will devote a whole chapter to balancing plans and sharing resources between teams but for now we just want you to get the idea that you plan work, you plan time and then you decide what to do with the surplus or shortfall.

Any questions?

We have shown the planning balance sheet at the level of a weekly summary to make it easy to see what is going on. Nearly all of the operations we work with actually break their weekly plan down to forecast the work in and work out on a daily basis and identify daily imbalances in work and time. This may sound a bit daunting, but modern software (like Workware™) make this task very easy, not only doing all the basic mathematics for you but also providing tools to help forecast future demand, to estimate what productivity to plan at and much more.

How many tasks?

That is entirely up to you and will be a pretty unique feature in every operation. What we would say is try to avoid the temptation of having too many tasks. People like 'granularity' when they are producing reports. More and more detail seems great. It helps to understand and explain performance. The problem with having lots of tasks is there is lots to plan. If your plans become unwieldy then your teams won't plan and all you will have is a very granular reporting system. (And having an ultra-wide, high-definition rear-view mirror will still not help you drive further or faster!)

Remember, the emphasis is on budgeting time so that people can get the work done. Bundle tasks together if they take similar times and your planning won't suffer too much. Better to have a plan that is roughly right so that you can act upon it than have no plan at all because it would have taken too long to produce it.

If you pressed us for a number, we'd say ten to a dozen tasks is a good range. Less than that and you may be glossing over some detail. More than that and creating the plan may become too time-consuming.

What goes into diverted activity?

We are talking here about things like meetings, training, coaching sessions and so on that add value to the business. They nurture and develop the team and co-ordinate activity. Don't be tempted to make this list too long. A team in one of our clients spotted that they could make their productivity reports look better if they said they had done more diverted activity. This is simply because we calculate how much time was spent on the work by starting with how much time was spent in the office and then subtracting the diverted activity (like training). The team started to brainstorm all of the things they could legitimately say that they had been doing that had distracted them from doing work. Tasks like filling the photocopier and emptying the confidential waste had found their way onto the list but the point at which we said (with considerable incredulity) 'Really!?' was when they added *catching spiders* to the list. 'It happens more often than you think...' was the case for the defence.

What had happened with this team was that they have developed an understandable, but mistaken, fixation on making productivity look good. Understandable because so often productivity had been used in the past to judge people so they wanted it to reflect them in the best possible light. But mistaken because we were using productivity to tune the system, not to punish or praise the individual. This meant we needed it to have a functional level of accuracy that would help to make plans realistic but not such a fine granularity that absolutely everything was put under a stopwatch.

So, put what you like down for diverted activity using the rule of thumb that they are important activities worthy of you planning for them to happen a week next Wednesday. Try to avoid the list growing to include any of the following:

- Going to the toilet. We really aren't interested.
- Talking about the football game, taking a smoking break, gossiping. It happens; get over it.
- The computer went down. If the computer goes down and someone sits staring at the screen, one can hardly call that an activity. Ask people what they did while the computer was down. If they didn't or couldn't do anything, then it is important to show that productivity was low as a result of poor IT systems.
- Catching spiders, rodents or any other office-based vermin.

Summary

This chapter has introduced the idea of the planning balance sheet and shown you what the core elements on both sides are.

We put *Core Work* (that is, customer facing) and *Diverted Activity* (important internal stuff that diverts us from directly serving the customer) on one side of the balance sheet. On the other side, we put the time that the team is paid for and then add or subtract from this when time is lost, or additional time is bought.

We have shown how the tasks that make up core work can be added together using a common currency to give us a budget for the time required in standard hours to get the work done. In the next chapter, we will go into much greater detail about how to plan each individual task.

Chapter 13

Planning work

The cost of service

There is a Marks & Spencer Simply Food outlet in Reading Station near to our UK office. The shop has four tills (at this time they were staffed by real people, and not self-checkout) and sells everything from a decent bottle of wine to a packet of nuts. This provides a useful illustration of how to manage the cost of service.

Imagine that there is a fairly steady flow of customers coming up to the tills and it is your job to ensure that those customers are served in good time. If you put one member of staff on Till 1 only, then a queue would start to form. If the queue isn't too long, people will wait. The sandwiches are pretty good after all, but if the queue gets too long then those sandwiches might get abandoned in favour of a short walk to the next shop. You could avoid having a queue at all by having staff sit at all four tills. A lot of the time those staff would have nothing to do (that is, they would have low utilization) but at least every customer walking up would not have to queue.

This is a basic trade-off in operations: carry the cost of employing people at low utilization to ensure high levels of service (in this case, getting to a check-out immediately), or try to optimize cost by creating an acceptable queuing time. This is what is going on when an operation sets a *service-level agreement* (SLA) such as processing an application in three days. It isn't because someone is going to slave over that application for a straight 72 hours; it is because having a small queue of work makes it possible to employ a smaller number of reasonably busy people rather than have a larger number of people virtually waiting around to pounce on the next application.

Actually, our observation of this M&S branch (and other retailers) suggests they have a perfectly elegant solution to this conundrum that we don't see enough of in back-office service operations. The Simply Food shop in the station will often have one person on the check-out and two or three other people doing stuff in the store: shelf filling, stock taking, tidying up. If a queue starts to build up, the person on the check-out rings a bell and someone stops what they are doing and opens up another till.

Stopping doing a less time-critical job to focus on the more immediate customer service demand is a way of blending different types of work together to get an optimum balance of cost and service. Do you do this where you work? Or do you find that the really time-critical stuff like answering phone calls is split off into a contact centre somewhere, while some of the back-office stuff (that could wait a day or two) is done somewhere else?

***

This chapter is going to take you into some of the intricacies of planning work.

Cost may not always be your biggest concern when it comes to customer service, but even if cost isn't top of your agenda, it doesn't make sense to spend resources on any given task if you don't have to. We are going to show you how to plan work in a way that makes sure that you use sufficient resources to meet your customer service targets while not tying up resources unnecessarily when they could be usefully doing something else.

There are two factors to consider when thinking about how much resources (or cost) to commit to a given task. These factors are your service-level target and the volatility of the work coming in from the customer. All will be explained below.

Service-level targets

Our M&S example gives you the idea that there is a relationship between cost and service: if you have to process all of your work the moment it arrives, then this will be like the shop putting someone on every till just in case someone needs serving. You would have to have enough staff to cope with peak demand. This will be more costly than if you can allow small queues of work to build up.

Whether or not this is possible depends on the nature of your business but we have found that nearly all operations we have worked with have some work that is less time sensitive than other work. Where operations remain determined to do non-time-sensitive work the instant it arrives, they will be adding cost, or tying up resources that could be used to provide better customer service in other ways. For this reason, we are going to go into some detail on how to plan for that less time-sensitive work so you can deliver service without using more resources than you have to.

Volatility of work

The cost of processing work will depend, in part, on how responsive you have to be, but also depends on how *volatile* your workload is. We're not suggesting you might be processing nuclear waste or anything; we mean how varied the demand from customers is from day to day, or minute to minute.

This is best illustrated with a quick example. Imagine you are planning complaint resolutions. Take a look at the following two patterns of work.

Pattern 1: Low Volatility

Day	Monday	Tuesday	Wednesday	Thursday	Friday	Totals	Average per day
Forecast work in	10	10	10	10	10	50	10

Pattern 2: High Volatility

Day	Monday	Tuesday	Wednesday	Thursday	Friday	Totals	Average per day
Forecast work in	15	12	5	8	10	50	10

In both cases, you are averaging ten complaints a day but the two patterns are very different. In Pattern 1, it is easy to know how much time you need to budget to do the task once you know the standard time and your team's productivity. But what about Pattern 2?

If the work had to be completed on the date of arrival, you would need to employ more time on Monday and significantly less time on Wednesday. Could your staffing patterns cope with this, or would you have to 'overstaff' for the whole week just to cope with the highest volume of work?

Maybe you could, but what if the work coming in is so volatile that not only does the volume fluctuate a lot from one day to the next but also you don't know when the high volume is going to come in? You would have to staff to a theoretical maximum level to be sure of getting the work done. (You may remember we talked about this in Chapter 3.)

Now, consider the difference if the work in Pattern 2 did not need to be done immediately but could wait for up to two days. You could imagine the following scenario:

- Do 10 complaints on Monday, carrying 5 over to Tuesday.
- Tuesday now has 17 complaints to do (the 5 carried and the 12 new), but again just do 10 and carry 7.
- Wednesday is now 7 plus 5 giving us 12 to do. Do 10 and carry 2.
- Thursday you have to do the 2 carried plus the 8 new work. Do all 10.
- Friday do all 10.

Now all the complaints have been resolved, with some being carried over from one day to the next. We have done it with the staffing required to do 10 items, rather than employing enough staff to do 15 or more.

Hopefully this shows you that you need to look at your work in terms of both volatility and desired level of service. High volatility (big fluctuations in workload coupled with unpredictability) and a need for a very rapid turnaround will inevitably be most costly. Low or predictable variation and slower turnaround acceptable will be less costly.

Using WIP to beat down the costs

That's WIP (*work in progress*) not 'whip' (we are still not recommending beating staff to improve performance) although 'whip' is how most people pronounce it.

We should stress again that when we talk about keeping costs down, we are not necessarily talking about taking cost out of the business. That may or may not be your priority. Our point is only that it doesn't make sense to tie up cost (or to be more accurate, people) unnecessarily when that same cost or resource could be adding value elsewhere in the operation.

In the example above, we talked about carrying some work from one day to the next so that we didn't need to overstaff to meet the peak demand. When we talk about carrying work over like this, we call it WIP. Think of it as being a way of smoothing the flow of work to create a nice even pace. People use different words for work that is not completed immediately: WIP, carry over, backlog. We prefer to use WIP in the positive sense of carrying work, *within service level*, that we are using to smooth demand. We use backlog to refer to work that has not been completed and has fallen outside of your service standards. So WIP is okay; backlog is not.

Work In	Work in Progress	Work Out
Work in is volatile and unpredictable	WIP rises or falls to absorb the variation	Work out is smooth(ish) giving people a calmer and more predictable pattern of work

Remember Reactive Ronnie? How stressful it must be to work for someone who is just constantly reacting to unpredictable events. First rushing like crazy and then sitting around with not enough to do. Using WIP you can smooth out the swings between panic and boredom. For this reason, we recommend (where possible) that you separate the planning process into two distinct parts:

- First, forecast how much work you are expecting to come in.
- Second, consider how much WIP you can carry and then use that information to determine how much work you plan to get done.

Back to our example above, a plan that uses 'WIP smoothing' would look like this:

Day	Monday	Tuesday	Wednesday	Thursday	Friday
WIP brought forward	0	5	7	2	0
Forecast work in	15	12	5	8	10
Total work available	15	17	12	10	10
Planned work output	10	10	10	10	10
WIP carried forward	5	7	2	0	0

You would forecast the *work in* in the first highlighted row and plan the *work output* in the second highlighted row. For example, you expect 15 items of work to come in (that's the forecast) and you intend to process 10 of those items (that's the plan). Forecasting is about expectation; planning is about intention. Sometimes they are one and the same, but often there is a difference. A very important difference.

You can see that in this plan, the two highlighted lines are what you have to focus on; the amount of WIP is calculated from the sums.

Unless you are an Excel genius, this might look a bit daunting but, once again, we can reassure you that there is software to take care of this for you. Do get in touch with us if you want help with this. All you need to know right now is why it is important to plan WIP if your service-level agreements allow you to.

WIP as a 'head of work'

We have just been talking about how WIP helps us to smooth demand and give people an even flow of work. This is only possible if our service levels allow us to carry work over from one day to the next, and this should be defined by what it right for the customer not just what is convenient for you.

Another way to look at the benefits of carrying WIP is that it gives you a 'head of work': something to draw from which means the people don't run out of work and grind to a halt. In the above example, you can see that Wednesday would be rather quiet if the team had enough people to process ten complaints but there were only five available to work on. Carrying some work from Tuesday into Wednesday means that the team will be better utilized on the Wednesday.

WIP works as a buffer, not only to ensure you don't have to staff up to peak workloads (or stress people out working too hard), but also to ensure that you don't run out of work or carry unused cost if things go quiet.

This begs the question: what is an appropriate level of WIP? If you carry too much then customer service will be compromised; if you carry too little, then you risk running out of work. Let's say that our customer service charter commits us to responding to all complaints within three days. What is the right amount of WIP? If only someone had come up with a way of calculating this…

… Cue John Dutton Conant Little from the Massachusetts Institute of Technology.

Little's Law

We are going to play a little fast and loose with Mr Little's law here, and any professors of queuing theory or masters in probability theory should look away now. All we are interested in is the beautifully simple underlying idea of this 'law' and how it helps us to plan.

Simply put, the law tells us that the *number of work items in a system is equal to the average arrival rate of the work multiplied by the average time that work stays in the system.* (For example, if you have an arrival rate of ten complaints a day and it takes three days to process them, then you would have 30 complaints in the system at any one time.)

Think back to our M&S outlet at Reading Station. People come into the store in ones and twos, look around and choose their stuff, queue up to pay then leave, while more people are arriving. Arrive, queue, leave; arrive, queue, leave. There will be a flow rate of people arriving and leaving. If people are arriving faster than they leave then the store will fill up and vice versa, it will empty. This 'system' (the store) is said to be 'stationary' when the rate of people arriving and leaving are the same. Let's say that 120 people enter the store between 12:00 and 13:00 to get their lunchtime snacks. That is, on average, two people every minute enter the store, while a different two people are heading out the exit with their pot of super-nutty wholefood salad. So how many people are in the shop at any one time?

If we say that people spend about five minutes in the shop, choosing their foods, queuing and paying for it, then there will be around ten people in the shop at any one time.

Obviously, it is not quite as ordered as in this illustration, but this may help you picture the scene.

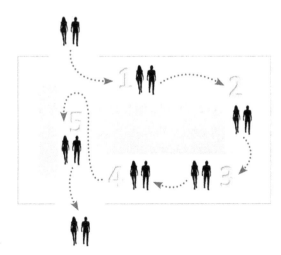

Think of a beat every minute with two people entering, two leaving and everyone else moving round one stop.

That is an average flow rate of two per minute, a wait time of five minutes and $2 \times 5 = 10$ people in the system.

What has this got to do with claims processing, mortgage handling or any other service operation? Well it helps us to work out what the desired level of WIP would be when we are planning our work.

Back to our complaints resolution example. An average of ten complaints a day and a commitment to resolve all complaints in three days. That gives us a maximum WIP of 30 complaints. If we have more than 30 in hand, then there is a very strong chance that we are failing our customer charter.

10 complaints in	10 (day 1)	
	10 (day 2)	
	10 (day 3)	10 complaints out

Okay so far? We need to take one more step before you have the full picture on how to plan work the AOM way. Consider for a moment which is worse: failing your customers and missing your customer charter of resolving complaints within three days, or running low on work to do and having a couple of slightly less productive days?

Clearly, the customer comes first so we should err on the side of caution. We should set a target level of WIP that means we will be pretty certain of always meeting our service levels. This target level is what we call a policy stock.

Policy stocks

There is no exactly right figure for this, other than a number that is slightly less than the one calculated by Little's Law, but there are a couple of things to take into account that will help you to decide.

Can you see a flaw in the picture with the stack of complaints? It has forgotten everything we said earlier in this chapter about volatility. There might be an average of ten complaints a day, but in reality our example suggested it could be anything from five to 15 complaints. This is why using the figure of WIP strictly from Little's Law is risky. If we had that surge of 15 complaints (50% more than the average), we might not be able to respond quickly enough to stay within our service targets.

So you want to set a target for policy stock a bit lower than the number from Little's Law. How much lower will depend on two things: how much volatility there is in the pattern of work coming in and how big a deal it would be if you missed your target.

A little below Little's Law if...	A lot below Little's Law if...
• Work is not very volatile (it is always quite close to the average)	• Work if very volatile (it is often a lot more or less than the average)
It doesn't matter too much if the service-level target is breached (e.g. if it is an internal target, not customer facing).	It is a big deal to miss the service-level target (you would be letting customers down).

Returning to our complaints department one last time then. Little's Law gives us a maximum WIP of 30, but we have quite a volatile intake of work and these are customers who are already not impressed with us so we don't want to risk missing our commitments. Let's set our policy stock at 25 complaints, not 30. Here's how this would work in a couple of planning scenarios.

Getting back down to policy stock

If something had gone wrong last week and, as we sit down to plan next week, we know that we have 50 unanswered complaints in hand, we need to plan to get that number back down to the more manageable figure of 25.

Let's say that we know the work is volatile but we really don't have any idea which days are going to get more or less complaints so we plan on a forecast of the average of ten complaints a day coming in. We now have two options for trying to get our WIP back down to the policy level of 25:

1. Plan to handle 35 complaints on Monday. This is based on having 50 outstanding plus another 10 new complaints arriving and wanting to end up with 25 by the end of the day.
2. Plan to handle 15 complaints every day next week. If getting back down to policy stock on one day would be difficult because you don't have the staff, this is a smoother way to do it. By planning to 15 a day you will be reducing the WIP by five every day of the week. 10 in 15 out. That is a reduction on the starting WIP of 50 by 25 over the course of the week.

In the second scenario, your plan for this task would look like this:

Day	Monday	Tuesday	Wednesday	Thursday	Friday
WIP brought forward	50	45	40	35	30
Forecast work in	10	10	10	10	10
Total work available	60	55	50	45	40
Planned work output	15	15	15	15	15
WIP carried forward	45	40	35	30	25

This is active management at its best: no panic, no knee-jerk over-reaction, just a smooth and calm steadying of the ship. Getting ourselves back into a positive position that we know puts us in control.

So finally, and this one might cause a few arguments:

What if you had a great week last week and the WIP had fallen well below the policy stock of 25? Let's say you cleared them all out and the WIP to be brought forward to next week is zero. Now what do you plan?

The instinctive answer is probably to keep it at zero. Why not? That's better customer service. Yes, it is and under certain circumstances that may be exactly the right decision but if you do decide to keep the WIP at zero, you are also deciding (albeit implicitly) to:

- not release some of the complaint handling resources to do something else (like help another team, do some training, or whatever);
- risk running out of work on complaints during the week and have lower productivity (and higher unit cost for complaint handling) because you have kept people around unnecessarily.

The choice is yours, of course; we just say it should be a conscious choice based on all the options being clearly available. Here is what you could plan:

Day	Monday	Tuesday	Wednesday	Thursday	Friday
WIP brought forward	0	5	10	15	20
Forecast work in	10	10	10	10	10
Total work available	10	15	20	25	30
Planned work output	5	5	5	5	5
WIP carried forward	5	10	15	20	25

This plan releases 50% of the capacity of the complaints handling team while you rebuild that small head of work that will help the team to run most efficiently.

It's all in the blend

We have focused quite heavily on setting policy stocks and planning to meet them but we can't leave this chapter without returning to the point that not all work can, or should, carry stock in this way. You can't have stock of unanswered phone calls or, if you have a share-dealing team, then you must complete the transactions at the deadline.

Any work that has to be completed within the day, hour or minute cannot carry stock. This means, as we suggested at the start of the chapter, that with these tasks you are more likely to have to plan for the maximum level of resources (and a bit more if the work is very volatile) and accept the cost of low utilization of your people. But you can do what we saw in M&S and blend some of the resources you have between the more time-critical and the less time-critical work.

Using your policy stocks wisely on the work that *can* carry WIP means you can move people on and off of this work to make sure that you get all the 'same-day' work done without having to be highly inefficient. Blending together work with different service targets has been a huge opportunity for performance improvement in a lot of the places we have advised. It takes a while and often involves a certain amount of cross-training and breaking down some cultural and structural barriers. You may not be able to do this immediately (or you might already be doing it – in which case, can we come and visit?) but it is worth seeing this as a destination.

Summary

There has been a lot in this chapter but if you are a department manager or someone else in a role that will have to support a number of team leaders in their efforts to produce plans, then understanding policy stocks and how to blend different types of work together is critical to delivering the best possible service within your budget. If you can grasp these principles, then you will be able to help your team leaders to help their teams to deliver the best possible balance of cost, quality and service.

In this chapter, we have focused on planning a specific task. The previous chapter took a higher-level view of the whole 'planning balance sheet' where all of these tasks were added together (using a common currency). As we move into the next chapter, we will return to that higher-level view and assume that you (or your teams) have done all of the task-level planning and are now getting together to look at the balance sheet in total.

What if the balance sheet isn't balanced?

Chapter 14
Balancing a plan

Nobody wins unless everybody wins

This is one of those 'I wish I had said that' phrases. In many ways, it perfectly sums up the principles of AOM. It captures the ideas of co-operation, supporting colleagues, being successful. But we can't claim credit for these words of wisdom. It was actually something that Bruce Springsteen used to say to his audience during live performances of his *Born in the U.S.A.* tour in the 1980s. Bruce was none too impressed with the way Ronald Reagan and his election team had tried to reference his works as a sort of upbeat American anthem. Our understanding is that the title track 'Born in the U.S.A.' was actually about a small-town criminal who got shipped off to Vietnam and came back with PTSD. Bruce wanted to put out a message about fairness and equality.

Our message might not quite have the social conscience as that intended by The Boss, but the sentiment holds true in a way for operations, and AOM tries to make sure that every person, every team and every department 'wins' in terms of delivering service to the customer.

Often people talk about 'silos' in operations, or a 'silo mentality'. It sometimes seems as though there are invisible but impenetrable walls between units of the operation that lead to teams or departments focusing only on *their* own targets, *their* own customers. This risks driving a 'win at all costs', or 'beggar my neighbour' culture. It can become hard to remember that the operation is one entity with a shared purpose and that all customers are everybody's customers.

Think about your own organization. Are your teams likely to achieve more, and give better service to all customers, if they compete with one another? How well do your teams co-operate? How well is your overall department able to work with other departments? It may feel like the structures placed around you, and the targets placed upon you, force this silo thinking and internal competition. We urge you to look past that and strive to foster co-operation for the greater good of the whole operation. You will win when you are helping everybody to win.

It is rarely the case that overachieving in one team counterbalances failing in another team. Imagine this conversation at the Leeds branch of Safe Hands Insurance: 'I'm sorry we missed our target date to settle your claim, Mr Rigsby, but on the plus side, all claims in Manchester were paid early last month.'

If we accept that for a given operation, Success + Failure = Failure, then the onus must shift from seeking success only within one silo to asking how we manage the system of the operation to make it possible for every silo to succeed.

We saw how this can go wrong in one public-sector operation where they had extended the traditional 'RAG reports' (that is, red, amber, green) to RAGB reports. In their system, red meant failing a target, amber meant at risk of failing, green meant on target and blue meant beating the target. Teams would strive to get a blue rating. Any team showing blue on their reports would be indignant if they were asked to help out a team with an amber status, even though that could mean that both teams could report a green status.

What would teams in your operation do in these circumstances? Would they help everyone 'go green' or would they shoot for blue even if it meant others going red?

***

In this chapter, we are going to talk about balancing plans. That is to say: actively deciding what to do if you have too few resources to hit your targets *and* what to do if you have more than enough resources to hit your targets. As we have hinted in the opening to this chapter, one of the best ways of balancing plans is to share resources, or move work, between teams. This means you may have to thinks about breaking down silos and working across teams, departments, even geographic territories.

Before we get to this, we will look first at the question of 'why bother?': what is the impact of not balancing a plan? Then we will look at the choices your teams have when deciding what to do to balance their own plans and finally we will turn to the question of balancing resources across teams.

Why bother?

We talked a little about this in Chapter 12 when we first introduced the idea of the planning balance sheet. Remember our example:

WORK				TIME	
Core Work	**Standard**	**Target**	**Hours**	**Resources**	
Applications	20	300	100	Staff Complement	350
Phone calls	5	800	67	Downtime	
Emails	10	500	83	Sickness	0
Hours required at standard			250	Holiday	35
Productivity	80%				
Total hours required			313	Total hours available	315
				Balance	-15
Diverted Activity				**Actions**	
Training			14	Flexitime	
One-to-one			3	Overtime	
				Borrow	
Total hours required			330	Loan	

Here we are 15 hours' short but as we said before, this is not the time for the team leader to throw her hands in the air and say: 'Well, we'll just have to do the best we can.' Nor should the department manager be issuing some vague edict like 'failure is not an option'. (No really, we have seen that sort of behaviour! It is often wrapped in modern management speak like 'Bring me solutions, not problems' or 'We value "can-do" attitudes around here' but the effect is the same: to try to ignore data that doesn't tell the story you want to hear.)

Our point is that you can't wish the problem away; you have to plan the problem away. If you are in the role of department manager, it is vital to be coaching your team leaders to work with their teams, and with other teams, to solve problems.

If the week were to go ahead with the team leader knowing that the team needed 15 hours' more time to meet their targets, they might, just might, cope. But it is much more likely that something would have to give. If nothing else could be done about it, then not all of the work would get done, which would mean some sort of prioritization. Now that could be an active decision, taken by the team leader in consultation with the team, or it could effectively be taken on the hoof by individual team members depending on how overloaded they happen to be. Worst of all, the prioritization could be driven by the customer, with some more articulate or assertive customers getting better service by pushing harder than others. That can't, surely, be the best plan!

It is reasonably clear that if a team is short of the resources it needs to meet its customer service commitments, it should try to find additional resources – maybe delay some training or actively prioritize which work must get done. But what if the situation is reversed?

What if the plan had shown a 15-hour surplus? With more than enough time to do the work, customers will be satisfied, but without a plan those 15 hours could go to waste. (It would be futile, for example, to look back at the end of the week and say 'that would have been a good week to do some extra training'!) In our experience, the most common outcome, in unplanned environments, is that the time just slips through your fingers. The work gets done but everyone just works a little bit slower and easier. No one does this deliberately, or even notices, but people pace themselves to the demand. If you didn't need those 15 hours for anything else, you could say 'What's the problem?' but when was the last time you had the luxury of squandering time?

One of the core principles of AOM is *use it or lose it*. If you don't make use of time that you identify as available, you will most certainly lose it. You can't get time back.

The idea of planning ahead is to make sure that the surplus time is put to the best possible use, and that no one looks back at the end of the period and wishes they had done something different with the time.

Good and bad balancing decisions

What are the options when faced with a surplus or shortfall of time? Let's take a look, starting with what to do with a surplus of time.

Do more customer-facing work than planned. You exist to serve your customers so this might be the right answer and will improve customer service. On the other hand, we are assuming that you have put together a plan that meets all of your customer service targets and you *still* have some time left over. Overachieving on your targets may not be the best thing to do with that time; you could be helping someone else 'to win'.

Do more diverted activities. This may be a better option. Bring forward some training, get that data security briefing out of the way, do some work on team problem solving from any issues that you have stored up recently. Remember, one of the core principles of AOM is that prevention is better than cure, and time invested in improving things or developing the team could be just what is needed.

Loan some time to support another team. This is where we start to break down the walls of those silos and start to foster co-operation. It might involve offering to take work off another team or lending people to that team. Can you contribute to everybody winning? Remember: what goes around comes around. If you help out another team one week, they may return the favour another time.

What about dealing with a shortfall?

Doing less customer-facing work than planned. This should be a last resort. Serving the customer is always top priority, but if it is the only option open to a team, then it is still better to create a balanced plan than leave it unbalanced and hope for the best. At least that way you stay in control and make conscious choices. You may even be able to forewarn customers of a delay, which is much better than them just finding out when you don't deliver.

Planning and prioritizing in this way also has the benefit of supporting staff morale. It is rarely their fault if the team is short of resources and it makes no sense for them to feel the pressure of trying to meet an impossible target. Far from motivating them to stretch for the impossible, it is likely to lead (at least after the second or third time of asking) to performing less well and missing the target by even more as a sense of helplessness creeps in. To keep asking a team to achieve the impossible is, to us, like putting up that motivational poster that reads: 'The beatings will continue until morale improves.' The team should feel good about hitting a planned outcome, even if that does fall short of the ideal outcome.

Doing less diverted activity. This may be a better plan than reducing the amount of customer-facing work to be done, but we have to be careful not to get into a cycle of always cancelling training, putting off one-to-one coaching and so on. Diverted activities should be planned with good reason and so if your team leaders suggest cancelling them to balance their plan then you would be justified in asking just how important the activities were in the first place. Also ask: if not now, then when? Diverted activities are often associated with team maintenance and development: regularly cancelling these sends all the wrong signals.

Borrow some time from another team. This might involve exporting some work to another team or importing someone into the team with the shortfall. This can be where you really earn your corn. If the walls in the silos are particularly high, or if the targets strongly favour teams sub-optimizing, then persuading one team to help out another might be a challenge. Have courage! It does work. A team that borrows one week might lend resources another week. Favours build up, exchanges are made, trust grows. Everybody starts to win.

These are the main decision areas for teams looking to balance their work and resources. You may be able to think of others such as tinkering with flexi-time, if you have, that or offering overtime.

The loading meeting

We hear a lot of talk these days about team meetings. 'Agile', the currently popular methodology that grew out of computer programming, calls them scrum meetings. Others call them buzz meetings, shift meetings, team huddles… you may well have your own term.

Team meetings are great and we highly recommend them as part of the AOM process. It can, however, be a problem if meetings only happen at a team level. Focusing everything on the team can strengthen the walls of the silos and lead to sub-optimization. Remember: nobody wins unless everybody wins. As well as team-level meetings, there needs to be some sort of co-ordination meeting for collections of teams.

As we have just been suggesting, very often the best way to balance work and resources is to trade work or time between teams. This is where the idea of a loading meeting comes in, which brings together a number of related teams. This is still a team meeting of sorts but it is your team of team leaders. (Or if you have self-directed work teams then a representative from each team.)

Typically, a loading meeting will involve all the teams from a department (or whatever you call the next layer up in your hierarchy). It will be chaired by someone like you, who is responsible for the performance of a group of related teams.

The process for the meeting will go something like this:

1. On a Thursday morning, all your team leaders will start to plan for the following week. You might give them a steer on any priorities you know about, and they might get information from Marketing, Central Planning, or whatever other support structures you have, to give them some ideas about future volumes. Ideally the software they use will also give them information about trends and even offer guidance on forecast volumes.

    The team leader will also engage with their team to understand individual and collective agendas. Is anyone planning to take time off? Are there any known issues to take into account?

By late morning, the team leaders will all have an ideal plan. This should include planning to hit all service-level targets, keep up with training plans, account for known absences and so on. The plan will almost certainly not be balanced: there may be too many or too few resources to do it all but the team leaders should not try to correct this just yet.

2. Thursday afternoon you will convene a loading meeting with your team leaders where each of them will share their plans, explaining any assumptions or priorities. Most of the operations we work with either put all the information up on a whiteboard, or project it from a screen in their software. The idea is to create a collective view of challenges facing all of the teams as a whole. At that meeting, you may want to challenge certain assumptions but the main aim is to help create a dialogue among the team leaders with the objective of achieving the best use of resources available across all of the teams present.

   The most likely outcome will be that some decisions are made to move some work or resources between teams to try to balance things up as well as possible. It may not be perfect but it is likely to be better than if each team had just operated in its own silo.

3. Informed by decisions from the loading meeting, the team leaders will go back to their teams and finalize their plans. If they couldn't cover all of their shortfall of resources, or loan out all of their surpluses, they will decide with the team on how to balance up the plan from actions they can take themselves. This final, balanced plan will be the one that the team commits to delivering next week.

4. Generally, teams have a commitment meeting on a Friday where the final plan is discussed. That way, everyone goes home for the weekend knowing that next week is sorted. Okay, not everyone works an old-fashioned five-day week these days,

but hopefully you can see the intention here. People are kept involved, know that they are working towards an achievable outcome, and know what part they have to play in the next period to deliver that outcome.

Here is an example of what the whiteboard might look like at a commitment meeting:

Core Work

	Monday	Tuesday	Wednesday	Thursday	Friday	Weekly Plan
Applications	60	60	60	60	60	300
Phone calls	160	160	160	160	160	800
Emails	100	100	100	100	100	500

Diverted Activity

	Monday	Tuesday	Wednesday	Thursday	Friday	Weekly Plan
Training	7	7				14
One-to-one	3					3

Resources

	Monday	Tuesday	Wednesday	Thursday	Friday	Weekly Plan
Staff complement	70	70	70	70	70	350

Downtime

	Monday	Tuesday	Wednesday	Thursday	Friday	Weekly Plan
Sickness						0
Holiday	7	7	7	7	7	35

Actions

	Monday	Tuesday	Wednesday	Thursday	Friday	Weekly Plan
Flexitime						
Overtime						
Borrow	7	7				
Loan						

5. There are many variants of this and we like it when teams apply a little creativity to make the whiteboard their own, but there are some key features to note.

- This is a daily plan building towards a weekly total. That way, you can follow progress towards the plan.
- The numbers in the boxes are intended work volumes that the team has committed to. They are not simply a sub-set of corporate targets, or a forecast delivered by the Central Planning team (although that can be a helpful starting point). These figures should represent what the team genuinely feels it is able to do next week – assuming the work comes in as expected and no one takes a surprise duvet day in the middle of the week.
- In our simple example, every day is planned to have one-fifth of the week's workload, but you might know that the beginning of the week is always busy or that Fridays are manic. If that is the case, then that can be reflected in the plan.

As a department manager, you will be coaching your team leaders by asking them if the plan is a realistic reflection of what they expect to happen next week, and whether they and the team are committed to making it happen.

Helping everyone to win

This is perhaps one of the single most important roles for a department manager or anyone who has a number of teams working for them. Organizations naturally have to be divided up into smaller units, such as teams; it therefore falls to the leader at the next level up to try to stitch the whole thing back together again.

You can help your teams to win by helping them to co-operate; by creating the sense that all targets are everybody's targets, all customers are everybody's customers and nobody wins unless everybody wins.

Go out there and make Bruce proud!

Chapter 15

Controlling to plan

Richard visited a contact centre out in New Zealand in the early 2000s. The client was confident Richard would find a model of good practice. Service levels were high and customer satisfaction surveys always came back positive. After spending a few hours at the site, Richard could see why results were so good.

What he saw was a lot of agents with very little to do. Service was good because agents were almost queuing up to take the next call. When Richard discussed this with the local leadership, their response was that the Central Planning function typically overestimated their forecast of calls to be answered and also overestimated the 'shrinkage' value (that is, the amount of time that would be lost due to things like unexpected absence). As a result, the local leadership found themselves with more time available than was built into the plan, and this time was being made available to do less work than expected.

'Doesn't this bother you?' asked Richard.

'Not particularly' was the reply. 'We are measured on service level and we are hitting it. If the forecasters are getting their sums wrong, that's their problem.'

This is perhaps an extreme example of the passivity that can creep into teams that see the forecast as something to blame, rather than something to guide action.

- The team misses its service level: 'Not our fault – more work came in than forecast. There is no way we were geared up to do that much work.'
- The team misses its productivity goals: 'Not our fault – less work came in than forecast and we had people sitting idle.'

This is what can happen when people feel little or no ownership of the forecasts or plans that are handed to them.

Prediction versus adaptation

One of the main ways in which operations have tried to overcome unresponsiveness to inaccurate forecasts is to try harder and harder to make the forecasts more accurate. This rarely works. Algorithms get more complex and the technology driving the forecasts gets more specialized, leading to forecasts being done by central experts, creating a greater divide between the forecasters and the teams doing the work. Variations still occur and teams feel even less motivated to 'bail out' the computer model.

In short, there is often too much emphasis on prediction and not enough on adaptation. It is quite liberating to realize that the forecast probably won't be right and part of the front-line task is to respond to conditions as they emerge. There are not many jokes in the world of operations management (and even fewer good ones) but here is our favourite:

'There are only two types of forecast... lucky and wrong.'

We did say there weren't many good ones! The point here is that we feel it is unwise to put too much faith in forecasts. It makes you stiff and unresponsive. If you start off from the premise that the forecast is just a useful starting point to try to set you off in the right direction, but things may change, then you are much more likely to be unsurprised and ready to take corrective action when things don't turn out as expected.

While we do build a lot of intelligence into the forecasting algorithms of our software, this is to help front-line teams to come up with workable levels of accuracy for themselves. Also, we hope that people will always treat computer forecasts as 'decision support' not 'decision replacement'.

What we want to avoid is the equivalent of the 4×4 driver who tries heroically to follow their sat nav as it takes them up a road just wide enough for a small motorbike and sidecar. This is what can happen when we start to trust what we are told rather than the evidence before our eyes.

***

Robert Burns tells us that 'The best laid schemes o' mice an' men / Gang aft a-gley'. This chapter is about what to do when our best-laid plans do as Burns suggested they often do, and 'go awry'.

Back to our scenario: last Thursday, your team leaders put together plans, based on forecast volumes and anticipated staff availability. On Friday, they held commitment meetings with their teams but by Wednesday of this week things are looking very, very different. What should they be doing? This is what we are going to cover in this chapter.

1. Keep things visual
2. Use 'now-expected' planning
3. Always be optimizing.

Keeping things visual

In Chapter 3, on the principles of AOM, we talked about visual controls and said that one of our five core principles was to keep things 'in sight, in mind'. Let's have a look at what our planning whiteboard might look like by Wednesday morning.

Core Work

	Monday	Tuesday	Wednesday	Thursday	Friday	Weekly Plan
Applications	60 *40*	60 *50*	60	60	60	300
Phone calls	160 *120*	160 *120*	160	160	160	800
Emails	100 *80*	100 *90*	100	100	100	500

Diverted Activity

	Monday	Tuesday	Wednesday	Thursday	Friday	Weekly Plan
Training	7 *7*	7 *7*				14
One-to-one	3 *3*					3

Resources

	Monday	Tuesday	Wednesday	Thursday	Friday	Weekly Plan
Staff complement	70 *70*	70 *70*	70	70	70	350

Lost Time

	Monday	Tuesday	Wednesday	Thursday	Friday	Weekly Plan
Sickness						0
Holiday	7 *7*	7 *7*	7	7	7	35

Actions

	Monday	Tuesday	Wednesday	Thursday	Friday	Weekly Plan
Flexitime						
Overtime						
Borrow	7 *7*	7 *7*				
Loan						

We have now written in the actual figures achieved next to the plan and instantly you can see that there is less work coming in than planned. Since everything else has been done according to plan – the training and one-to-ones have been done, holiday taken, resources borrowed – this means that productivity for those two days *must* be lower than planned. Less work than planned has been done but it has been completed with the originally planned amount of resources.

What this should suggest to you is that Wednesday needs a little re-planning. Carry on as you are and it could be a costly week with a lot

of missed opportunity. You will experience what we talked about at the very start of the book: a surfeit of latent capacity. That is to say, capacity was available to add value to your business and your customers, but went unused.

Having the numbers up on a whiteboard helps to keep things visual and to focus the whole team on the variations. You can be creative with colour as well to highlight variations even more, such as writing short-falls to plan in red and surpluses in blue.

Now-expected planning

What would you say to a team leader if they learned nothing from these first two days but came to you at the end of the week and said: 'D'you know what boss? Last week would have been a great week to get some of that GDPR training done!'?

After two days of significant variance from plan, we should at the very least ask ourselves some pertinent questions. In particular:

- Is this a blip? Maybe volumes have been lower than planned for a couple of days but we might be certain that it is an anomaly and the rest of the week will return to what we planned.
- Is it a delay? Maybe we are pretty sure that the total amount of work for the week will still come out on plan, which means that volumes might actually go up for the rest of the week.
- Is it a trend? The most likely possibility is that the first two days give us a good idea of what is to come for the rest of the week. Volumes are down and will stay down for the rest of the week.

Once we have addressed these questions, we can start to re-set our expectations. Let us assume that the two days of lower work volumes is the start of a trend and we think that the volume will continue to be lower than planned for the rest of the week.

The following table shows what we might expect to happen on Wednesday, based on the first two days.

	Two days' planned	Two days' actual	Variance	% Variance	Wed plan	Now expected
Applications	120	90	-30	-25%	60	45
Phone calls	320	240	-80	-25%	160	120
Emails	200	170	-30	-15%	100	85

If you look at the *Applications* line, you can see that we expected 60 in on Monday and Tuesday. That's 120 over the two days, but actually we only received 40 on Monday and 50 on Tuesday. So that is 30 fewer than expected. A variance of 30 applications against an expectation of 120 is a difference of 25%.

It might therefore be reasonable to reduce our expectations for Wednesday. 25% of 60 is 15 so let's reduce our plan by that number. We have a now-expected figure of 45 applications for Wednesday.

In the table, we have applied the same logic to phone calls and emails.

The team leader can update their whiteboard on Wednesday morning before the team huddle and let everyone know that volumes of work are below plan and the team can agree what to do to make good use of the unexpectedly available time. This is what we mean when we talk about now-expected planning. Just like the Active Fuel Management in the Chevy, or Active Traffic Management around Birmingham, this feedback and constant adjustment is what makes management active.

Always be optimizing

Although we haven't shown the sums here, we can tell you that the now-expected workload amounts to about 13 fewer hours of work to be done on Wednesday. Do nothing and that would be like having nearly two people sitting idle for the day.

Turn that around and that is an opportunity for two days' extra training, or maybe two days' worth of returning an old favour and loaning some resources to another team. This is what we mean when we say always be optimizing. Take any newly available data, learn from it and modify the intentions for the day ahead accordingly. Eat, sleep, optimize, repeat.

Forgive us if we seem to be labouring a point here, but this goes right to the heart of the role you can play in helping your team leaders, your team of teams, to achieve peak performance. This is where the reasons for doing AOM set out in Part 1 and the principles behind AOM described in Part 2 come together with the practical things that you can do.

- In Part 1 we explained that fluctuating productivity is a result of not balancing the amount of work to be done with the right number of people to do the work. This leads to latent capacity, which is just a formal way of saying wasted time (or money).
- Stabilizing productivity and optimizing performance require us to understand that operations work like complex, human systems. This governs how we design operations management solutions that will work with the grain of the real world.
- Controlling complex systems relies on responsiveness (or agility if you like), which in turn relies on clear, accurate, rapid feedback loops that give you information in time to respond.

We have used the example here of workloads falling below plan because it shows up most clearly the cost of being passive and doing nothing, and so also the benefit of doing now-expected planning and taking action. It is worth us considering some of the other likely scenarios.

Potential variances and levers of control

What could go wrong and what can your team leaders do about it?

If we think back to our basic balance sheet, we can see where things might vary from plan. We could have more or less than planned...

Work	Resources
Core Work	Staff Complement
Task 1	*less*
Task 2	Holidays
Etc	Sickness
Diverted Activity	**Balance**
Activity 1	**Actions**
Activity 2	Flexitime
	Overtime
	Borrow
	Loan

1. work;
2. diverted activity;
3. time available.

We have talked about the case of less work than planned coming in but of course the opposite could also happen.

In some ways, diverted activity ought to be more predictable because it is in the gift of you and your team leaders. But training courses, for example, could get cancelled – releasing more time for other work. Or they could over-run.

Time available can be reduced by unexpected absence. Holidays should not come as a surprise (unless your company has a particularly liberal approach to employee time commitments), but there is always the possibility of some degree of lateness or sickness.

Time availability might also be affected by changes to the actions you have planned. Maybe you have planned some overtime, but can't get enough people to do it. Or perhaps Accounts agreed to loan you Fred and Ginger but then suddenly they were no longer available.

What all of this comes down to is that the plans that your team leaders so beautifully balanced at the end of last week can become unbalanced on each and every day of the current week. There could be a surplus or shortfall of resources on each day as it arrives.

The levers of control are pretty much the same as the factors we talked about in the previous chapter for balancing the plan. Here is a checklist for your team leaders.

Sudden and significant shortfall of resources	Sudden and significant surplus of resources
• Can any other team loan resource or take some work off your hands?	• Can you find a team that would gladly borrow some resources or give you some work to do?
• Can you delay any of the diverted activity?	• Is there any work that can be completed sooner than planned?
• Can you make up the time with flexi-time or overtime?	• Can you offer to 'pay back' any flexi-time, letting people go early?
• If all else fails, which tasks are least customer-sensitive to a short delay?	• If all else fails, find some additional diverted activity to do. There must be something.

The reason we have talked about 'sudden and significant' is because we don't want you to encourage your team leaders to obsess over the odd minute here and there. Variances need to be significant and actionable. That means that typically we are talking about a situation where the plan is now out by three to four hours or more. That is to say, when you need, or could release, a person for half a day.

Summary

Being good at controlling to plan is a core operational competence. This is not about trying to achieve rigid compliance to the plan in the face of changing circumstances; rather, it is about using the plan to help to navigate a team towards the best possible outcome as circumstances change.

As we have said before, this is not about 'command and control', old-fashioned dictatorial management but it is about being, and feeling, 'in control'. It is about teams controlling their destiny; not being at the mercy of events.

The better teams are at controlling to plan, the more they will achieve, with less effort and much, much less stress. In the next chapter we will look at how to review how well teams are doing at staying in control.

Chapter 16
Reviewing and learning

I'll have a double

Learning is so important we recommend you do it twice!

Indulge us for a moment as we introduce you to an idea from one of our all-time heroes: Chris Argyris (1923–2013). He was born in Newark, New Jersey and was a professor at both Yale and Harvard. He was particularly well known for his work on organizational behaviour and on learning organizations. His advice is simple, practical, common sense and has guided our approach to reviewing and learning. Here's a short quote from his Wikipedia entry just to show you what his approach was all about – and why we like him so much:

> Argyris believed that managers who treat people positively and as responsible adults will achieve productivity. Mature workers want additional responsibilities, variety of tasks, and the ability to participate in decisions. He also came to the conclusion that problems with employees are the result of mature personalities managed using outdated practices.[1]

We mention him because of what he has taught the world of management about using feedback and learning from what is happening. He popularized the understanding of *double-loop learning* and we are going to show you how this will take your performance improvement to a whole new level.

---

[1] 'Chris Argyris', Wikipedia entry. Available from https://en.wikipedia.org/wiki/Chris_Argyris [accessed 27 August 2020].

Here is a classic example of first single-loop, and then double-loop learning from our work with a UK insurance company.

The New Business team found itself falling behind on its service levels with a growing backlog of new customer applications. This was the result of an unusual increase in the number of incomplete application forms causing them to have to contact the customer for additional information. In seeking to reduce the backlog, a review was set up which showed that the process for capturing additional information was not very efficient and so the process was mapped, simplified and partly automated to improve process efficiency. That's the first loop. What has happened here is sometimes referred to as *doing things right*: making the process as simple and efficient as possible.

Simplifying the process for capturing additional information seems like a perfectly reasonable thing to do. It is asking: 'Are we doing things right?' Sometimes we need to ask: 'Are we doing the right thing?' Double-loop learning addresses this second question. Rather than improving the additional information process, should we eliminate altogether the need for the process?

On further examination, the New Business team found that another team, Broker Relations, had changed the incentive payments process for the broker network. This had incentivized the brokers to propose more customers, more quickly rather than waiting to complete all the paperwork. Rather than making 'additional information capture' more efficient, the team actually needed to work on making that whole process unnecessary by liaising with colleagues to redirect the efforts of the brokers back to providing more complete information in the first place.

Now we will look at how double-loop learning can help you plan and control the capacity of your operations. In the previous chapter, we talked about learning lessons during the week: after two days of lower volumes of work, we ask: is this a blip or a trend? Should we change what we are doing to optimize performance for the week?

Eat, sleep, optimize repeat.

This is single-loop learning. In pictorial form, it looks like this.

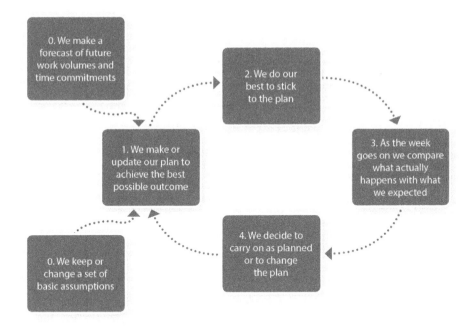

You will see that we have two starting boxes labelled 0 which feed into a simple cycle. We start by making forecasts about the future and have some basic assumptions which help us to take Step 1 of turning those forecasts into plans. (Remember: forecasts = expectations; plans = intentions.)

The single loop then continues as we try to follow the plan, we compare how we are doing against the plan and we make changes to the plan if necessary.

The most important assumptions that feeds into this loop are the assumptions made about 'standard times'. These help us to budget how much time we will need to do all the work necessary for our customers. For example, we have assumed that reviewing written applications will take 20 minutes, phone calls 5 minutes and emails 10 minutes.

On top of this we have assumed that our team, with its current levels of skills and experience, will work at 80% productivity.

These are the big assumptions and if they are wrong, the whole plan will be compromised. But there are plenty of other assumptions in there too: that Central Planning have given us a reasonably accurate forecast of customer demand; that sickness levels will be similar to what they have been in the past; that Colin from Accounts still hasn't replaced his goldfish. (If you haven't read Chapter 5 yet, that will make no sense whatsoever!)

The point is that with single-loop learning, we keep trying to optimize our performance *based on the assumptions as they stand*. Within a given week, this is fine, rational behaviour. Good active management. But if our plan keeps going awry, then we should start to question these basic assumptions. Questioning these assumptions is what gives us our second loop in double-loop learning.

Here's the full picture:

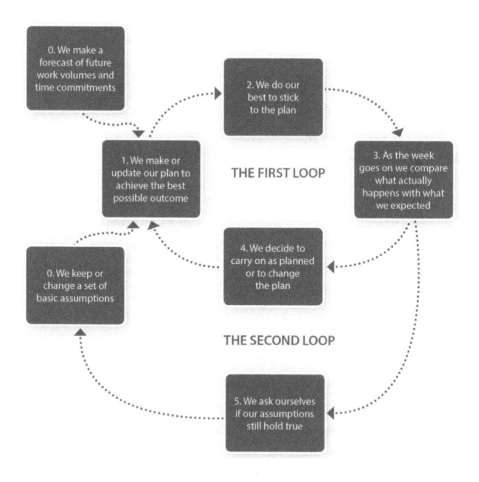

We have talked a lot about systems and how organizations can behave a little like natural systems, or ecosystems. Not that you have a lot of cane toads running around the office, but you do have complex interactions that can lead to unpredictable and unintended consequences.

To illustrate further, here is another example of a natural system showing how biology uses double loops to control a complex system.

Our body temperature needs to be carefully regulated for the chemical processes of the body to work correctly. We all know that the average body temperature is around 37°C. Even one degree either side of this can begin to feel uncomfortable and more than two degrees off and we can have serious problems. So it is essential that the body maintains its temperature with feedback loops.

If we get a little too cold, blood vessels constrict to conserve heat, sweat glands shut down and we may start to shiver. That's the first loop. A rapid, hard-wired response. The body does this itself. Getting up to put on a woolly jumper is the second loop. Now we have engaged slower thought processes, reviewed the situation and decided to do something about it.

In this context, you as a department manager or leader of teams influence the second loop. Your teams are like the reflex actions of the body: responding quickly to customer needs, making sure we do everything we can to stay on plan. This is important, and you may remember we said earlier that operations should always move control as close as possible to the customer, but it isn't enough to just have reflex actions like shivering when we are cold. We also have to engage the second loop of learning to improve our responses over time. You can focus attention on the second loop: how well did teams respond to changes? Do we need to review how we responded or do we need to review some of the assumptions that we have been making?

In this chapter we will now look at:

- The variance meeting where we challenge assumptions and learn lessons.
- The five most common variations from plan and how you can help teams to do double-loop learning to improve.
- The outline of a summary report that will give you all you need to run a variance meeting.

The variance meeting

There is a natural symmetry between the loading meeting and the variance meeting. In the first, you gather teams together to plan the best possible course of action for the next period. In the second, you look back at the period just finished and ask if there are any lessons to be learned.

Typically, a variance meeting will be held later on a Monday or on Tuesday morning when all of the previous week's data has been compiled. The agenda will involve each team leader, or representative, giving a short update and answering a few questions.

Each team leader will cover the following points in just a couple of minutes:

1. Workflow

   Did more or less work come in than forecast? Did we manage to stay on plan with the amount of work processed? Do we have more or less WIP to carry forward?

2. Team development

   Did we meet all our commitments for training and development, or for other internally focused work? If not, why not and when will it get done?

3. Resources

    Did everyone turn up as planned? Any unexpected absences and, if so, are we seeing a blip or a trend? Did we loan out resources we committed to, and did we receive any borrowed resources as agreed?

4. Performance

    Was productivity above or below plan? What was our highest and lowest day? Should we be thinking of changing our productivity in future plans?

5. Questions

    Any questions from other teams?

Variance meetings are a hugely important part of the whole process. They test and improve the planning discipline, give you a chance to identify new improvement opportunities and give everyone space to learn lessons together. But there is a risk that they seem to focus on negatives, such as why the plan was not achieved. (We had to smile but correct one of our clients when we discovered that their variance meeting was known locally as the Grilling Meeting. This was not our intention. Our aim is to create a safe environment for learning, not to put people on the spot.) This can be a real challenge for you, as someone likely to run such a session, and the key is to make sure that the focus is on creating that safe learning environment, where any variation is an opportunity to improve the process, not to find someone to blame. So not the Grilling Meeting, please!

You may have heard of *Black Box Thinking*, an idea popularized by Matthew Syed in his book of the same name. He argues that the key to success is a positive attitude to failure. We came across similar thinking to this many years ago when we were told about a computer company that had reinvented the old saying: 'To err is human, but to really foul things up you need a computer.' This company printed cards for all employees that started with 'To err is human...' on one side, but on the other side it said something like this: '...we expect you to make mistakes, but please make new ones. Old mistakes are boring, new ones, we can learn from.'

We urge you to take this attitude with your own teams. Clearly, protect everyone from making mistakes that would damage themselves, the company or the customers by following all appropriate regulations, but do encourage honest, fearless appraisal of where things go wrong.

One way you can support this is to know what insightful questions will help you to help others to reflect on how they did. Below we have listed the five most common patterns of variation from plan and suggested what questions these might prompt you to ask.

The big five variations

With each of the following five examples of variance from plan, you will have two basic questions in mind. The first is how responsive was the team leader to the emerging situation. In other words you are checking to see if they need any further support and coaching in how to run the first loop effectively. Your second question will be to ask if there are any lessons to learn from the variation to change our assumptions that feed into future plans. And that is the second loop.

Here are the big five.

1. Less work than planned and lower productivity

Getting less work than planned is forgivable: it just means that the forecast was wrong (rather than lucky). Not responding to it is less good. If you see a team that did less work and had lower productivity, it probably means that your team leader did not see the falling work volumes, and failed to respond in time to a growing availability of time to get something else done. They have simply kept the same level of resources to do one amount of work but used it to do less work.

Here you would be asking things like: When did you spot that work volumes were running behind plan? Did you identify any diverted activity that could be done? Were there any other teams that needed any help? Did you ask around?

This starts to address the responsiveness question, but then you may also need to ask: how long have work volumes been running below forecast? Is there something wrong with our forecasting assumptions? How are you changing your assumptions in next week's plan?

2. More work than planned and higher productivity

Sometimes this might happen on just one day or you might see it over a longer period of a week or more. Similar to number 1, this shows some lack of responsiveness: instead of finding additional resources to cope with the extra work, the team has had to work at a faster pace. This begs some really important questions:

- Were people being asked to work harder than is reasonable? One example could involve putting in longer hours but not recording them. This is not a true increase in productivity because more time has been spent to do the extra work – it just looks like higher productivity if the additional time is not being credited. At best, that is misleading; at worst, it is exploiting the workers unfairly.
- Were people having to cut corners to get the work done more quickly? Sometimes this takes the form of missing out steps in the process, which can lead to quality problems, or other times it can be done by 'cherry picking' the easier work. The latter strategy will generally lead to customer service problems while also piling up difficult work to be done another day.

- If the above two points do not apply, then should we assume that the level of productivity achieved was okay for the team? If the team can demonstrably work at a higher level of productivity than planned, then a new (higher) productivity target should be agreed for future work. This might seem harsh, like we are punishing people for doing a good job, but remember we are using productivity to help us estimate how much time to reserve to do the work. If we use a productivity figure that is too low, then we will fail to identify time that could be put towards training the team, helping out other teams, or serving more customers.

If you find that week after week a team's productivity keeps going up and up, then you might want to question the assumptions that went into the standard time for doing the work. For example, if a lot of teams are achieving 120% productivity with a standard time of 20 minutes for processing claims then maybe the standard time should be revised to, say, 15 minutes.

3. More sickness or other absence and less work done

People go sick from time to time; 'stuff happens' as they say (politely) so we just have to deal with this. The questions for the team leader, or team representative, to whom this has happened would focus first on responsiveness and second on assumptions.

- On responsiveness, we would be asking the team leader what steps they have taken to try to make sure that all the customer-facing work was done despite the unexpected absence. Was diverted activity prioritized? Were other teams asked for help? If it was not possible to do all of the work, then were steps taken to make sure that the work that was done was the highest priority?

- On assumptions, we would be asking the team leader to look at patterns of sick absence. This can be an early indicator of morale or wellbeing issues. Do we have a problem brewing? If so, why, and what can we do about it?

4. More sickness or other absence but the planned work (nearly) gets done so we had higher productivity

This is an interesting one. Let's take a really simple example: you have a team of ten people and two go sick but the eight people remaining do the work of nine people between them. On the one hand, the team has done less work than planned, but it is clearly not their fault (unless they somehow infected the two people who fell ill). It would be wrong to 'blame' the eight people who came in for missing a target set for ten people. Indeed, we might want to congratulate those eight for doing so well. Our double-loop learning leads us, again, to ask questions both about responsiveness and assumptions

- On responsiveness, this would be the same as the first point in number 3 above. What steps involved trying to make sure that all the customer-facing work was done despite the unexpected absence and was the work effectively prioritized?
- On assumptions, this would be done the same way as in number 2 above: what lessons can we learn from achieving higher productivity? Was it sustainable and can we plan at a higher level going forward? Are our standard time assumptions correct?

5. More time was unexpectedly available, no extra work done, so lower than planned productivity

This may seem unlikely but we have seen, for example, the sudden cancellation of a training course making additional time available.

Probably the most common extra time that becomes available is when high levels of contingency for sick leave are planned that don't reflect the day-to-day reality. Similarly, it is a common mistake to build in an allowance for holidays and assume that, say, 13% of paid time will be spent on holidays. If this is applied evenly in long-range plans then it will almost certainly be wrong. Headbanger Curt doesn't take 13% of each day off; he takes two weeks off in September to follow the rock festivals round Europe. When he's not packing his pop-up tent around sundry wet fields on the continent, he is in work for 100% of the day.

Over estimating holiday (and sick absence) by making simple assumptions is very common and can leave team leaders with more resources than expected so, once again, the question is what did they do with it? The questions are just the same (but for different reasons) as number 1: why wasn't the additional time put to good use, rather than allowing productivity to fall?

Critical comparisons

We first introduced the idea of critical comparisons in Chapter 8 when we asked you to imagine yourself sailing to the Cote d'Azur but going off course and nearly burning your engines out. Here we said that the way to lift *information* out of *data* was to incorporate three critical comparisons. We suggested that you compare actual performance to:

1. Planned performance
2. Performance over time
3. Standard assumptions about performance.

Here is what that might look like in a simple report, and it is this sort of report (a variance report) that we suggest you use to conduct variance meetings. We have highlighted where you can find each of the three comparisons. (Note for those with a keen eye for mathematics: the variances are rounded to the nearest 1%. So productivity going up from 80% to 85% is a five-point increase from 80. 5/80 = 6.25% and this is shown as 6% variance.)

ACTUAL OVER TIME						ACTUAL vs PLAN		
Core Work	Monday	Tuesday	Wednesday	Thursday	Friday	Plan	Actual	Variance
Applications	22	20	15	13	20	100	90	-10%
Phone calls	21	19	15	14	18	67	87	30%
Emails	17	16	12	14	16	83	75	-10%
Total						250	252	1%
Diverted Activity								
Training			7	7		14	14	0%
One-to-ones			3			3	3	0%
Total						17	17	0%
Resources								
Staff complement	70	70	70	70	70	350	350	0%
Downtime								
Sickness						0		
Holiday	7	7	7	7	7	35	35	0%
Actions								
Flexitime								
Overtime								
Borrow						15		-100%
Loan								
Performance								
Productivity	95%	87%	79%	73%	86%	80%	85%	6%
Utilization	100%	100%	84%	89%	100%	95%	95%	0%

ACTUAL vs STANDARD

There is a lot to take in on a report like this but if you read it systematically, you will very quickly get the hang of it.

Step 1: Look for key variations in actual versus plan

If you take a look at the right-most column, you will see three variations really stand out. The first this that this team processed 30% more phone calls than planned. Next, the team expected to borrow 15 hours from another team but this didn't materialize. Finally, productivity was planned at 80% but the team achieved 85%.

On closer inspection, the amount of core work processed was about right at 252 hours compared to a plan of 250, but the planned mix of work was wrong. Fewer applications and emails but more phone calls. We would discuss the implications for this for future planning: do adjustments need to be made to the forecasting models? Do we have the right balance of skills to do the work if the mix is very different? You get the idea.

Step 2: Look at the profile of work over time

A quick glance along the first few rows shows that the beginning and end of the week are typically busier than the middle. There is less work on Wednesday and Thursday in all work types. Quite sensibly, this team has carried out its training and one-to-ones on these quieter days.

Is this a general pattern or just a one-off? Are we taking account of this in our planning?

Step 3: Look at performance against standard assumptions

The key one here is the productivity. The planned productivity represents an assumption about how closely the team can perform to the standard times that have been used to convert the volumes of work into a budgeted amount of time. (Look back at Chapter 11 for a fuller explanation of this.)

As we have already noted, the team has performed at a higher productivity than expected. Why was this? They did just about the planned amount of work but had to do it in less than the planned amount of time (because the borrowed resources didn't turn up). So first off, well done team! Next, why was the loan of two people not forthcoming? Is there anything we should learn from this?

Finally, let's take a look at the productivity line near the bottom of the table, which shows what level of productivity was achieved on a daily basis. Here we see a whopping 95% productivity was achieved on Monday. This is much higher than the plan of 80%. This was a busier day than other days of the week and so the team had to deliver higher productivity. As we suggested earlier in the chapter, this begs a couple of questions:

- Was this level of productivity achieved by people working harder than planned? For example, putting in extra time that hasn't been logged somehow?
- Is 95% a sustainable level of productivity for this team, or are we forcing them to cut corners?
- If this is a sustainable level of productivity, then how should we factor this into future plans?

Right back at the beginning of the book, we talked about fluctuating productivity and here we are seeing it in action in a summary report of performance. Productivity has swung from 95% on Monday to 73% on Thursday. You may recall that we said that there are a number of problems with large variations in productivity. It is not a great way to get the best out of people; a smooth, even flow is much more effective and a lot less stressful. It also results in a more costly enterprise since each of the low-productivity days represents a lost opportunity – either to do more work for the customer or to use more time for internal development.

Summary

This chapter has been about how to build a set of teams that can learn and respond. This is absolutely fundamental to active management. Get your leaders to embrace the value of mistakes as routes to learning – rather than things to cover up and avoid. Making this work requires great leadership from you. Create a process that focuses on learning not blaming; coach people to improve, tolerate mistakes but not repeat mistakes.

This ends Part 3 where we have walked through the cycle of Forecast, Plan, Control and Review (and repeat). This should be enough to get you started helping your teams to manage more actively. We also offer a number of tools and tips online to help you to take this further, but for now we will leave the day-to-day work behind and step out to look at what the future holds of operations such as yours in Part 4.

Part 4

AOM and the bigger picture

W e know that AOM won't be the only thing, or the most important thing, in your life so we use this last part to put AOM in the context of other things that you are likely to be involved in, or may be going on around you.

Chapter 17 discusses where your operation might spend its 'performance improvement pound', acknowledging that AOM is not the only game in town and setting out what else we think is big news at the moment.

Chapter 18 describes some of the major change programmes that are common in operations like yours at this time. We cover: Lean, Agile, leadership development and empowerment.

Chapter 19 looks into the near future and considers some of the changing contexts for leaders like you. We consider: the gig economy, remote working and the rise of robots.

Chapter 20 wraps everything up and gives you a few pointers as to where to go to get more help and ideas.

Chapter 17
Where next?

The story so far...

As we move into the final part of the book, we feel it is time for a bit of a recap before we go on to look at the future of operations and how AOM may fit into the changing world you are working in.

We have written this book in four parts:

- Why?
- What?
- How?
- Where next?

In Part 1, we set out the reasons why you need AOM (or something like it) to help you control your operations. Depending on the size of your operation and exactly where you fit in, you may have more or less say over what changes can be made to your operation, but we believe anyone can implement at least some of the ideas behind AOM and can make a big difference.

- The pace and scale of change in operations means that it is more important than ever to have simple and effective controls in place to help you to optimize performance.
- Whatever the pace of automation, we believe that people will remain a key part of the equation for a long time to come and so a people-oriented method like AOM is most likely to help you to succeed.

- AOM helps you to turn latent capacity into useable capacity. It does this by helping you to achieve peak performance more often.
- Releasing latent capacity will reduce costs (if that is what you need to do) but it will also help you play your part in delivering the strategic changes required by your organization to survive and thrive in the future.

In Part 2, we began to explain the ideas behind AOM and to give you some of the core principles that would help you to refine and adapt the AOM methods to work for you.

- Organizations are complex human systems.
- Addressing the 'human' part of the operation is vital for success. Treating people with respect and working with them like adults will produce maximum performance.
- Managing complex systems is best done by accepting the liberating notion that no one will ever predict the future correctly all the time, or produce the perfect plan. As soon as this is accepted, the emphasis switches from improving prediction to improving responsiveness.
- Responsiveness comes in the form of feedback loops and AOM is designed to make these loops work for different time horizons and over layers of management in a cycle composed of forecasting (what you expect to happen), planning (what you intend to do about it), controlling (how you respond when things go off plan), and reviewing (how well you did so you can do better next time).

Part 3 offered you some practical steps to start to put the AOM ideas into action.

- Time can be used as a common currency to add together work of very differing characteristics. This helps you to budget how much time needs to be reserved to help teams deliver to the customer. Note: times in this context are not there to force people to work to the beat of the drum, or to drive piecework pay systems.

- Planning involves developing a simple balance sheet with work on one side and resources on the other.
- Understanding service requirements can help you to blend different types of work (like the staff in the Simply Food branch at Reading Station) to smooth the flow of work and to use resources most efficiently.
- Balancing plans requires you to come up a level (or two) from the team; to break down silos if they exist, and get people working together. Nobody wins unless everybody wins.
- Controlling to plan involves identifying emerging trends and updating plans with now-expected figures. This forms the first of two loops.
- Reviewing performance and discussing that at a variance meeting helps you to turn both success and failure (to deliver to plan) into lessons that will help you and your teams to do even better next time. Eat, sleep, improve, repeat.

Our intention here has been enough to whet your appetite and get you started on your AOM journey. Plans, commitment meetings, summary reports and variance meetings will all vary slightly from one place to another and you will have to work out what is right for you. This is why we have given you as much background as we can on 'the why'. That will help you to make the best design decisions for yourself. We are also out here and very happy to help!

No initiative is an island

We have aimed this book squarely at department managers: people who lead teams of teams. You are the engine room of change in your operations. It is up to you to keep the day-to-day service going while tactical and strategic initiatives are launched, implemented, evaluated, terminated, relaunched and so on.

We recognize therefore that at no time would the introduction of AOM be the only initiative on your agenda. At best this would just be one piece of a much bigger jigsaw puzzle. You may be faced with some relatively routine stuff like on-boarding new products and services, training up the staff, getting the procedures documented, and figuring out how many people you are going to need. On the other hand, you could be engaged in a wholesale restructuring and be realigning teams, centralizing some things while decentralizing, offshoring or outsourcing others. At times you might just want to scream 'STOP!' at the top of your voice. 'Just give me five minutes to think...'

But of course, that's not going to happen. The changes will keep coming and the customers will still need serving. Some used to say it felt like changing the wheel of a car while driving along the motorway. Now it probably feels like changing all four wheels while competing in a Formula 1 Grand Prix.

In Part 1, we said that AOM was part of the solution to this. AOM helps you to keep the day-to-day management of the operation simple, predictable and in control. When you have very little control, your attention is likely to be focused on the very short term: today, or maybe even on fixing yesterday's problems. As your level of control increases you will find yourself more able to focus on the future: the tactical and the strategic. If you want to be getting on, you will want to be looking upwards and outwards, not inwards and downwards. Forwards, not backwards.

AOM delivers capacity, control and choice.

So far, so good, but we know that if you are going to spend your precious time and attention on AOM then you need to know how it fits in with everything else in your world.

There are two questions to ponder here. The first concerns where to place your bets among all the competing initiatives available to you and the second concerns what the near future holds for you in such a rapidly changing world.

Spending the performance improvement pound

Chapter 18 will deal with the question of alternatives. Imagine your CFO has her performance improvement pound to spend (…or dollar, rand, whichever). She will want to get the best she can from that pound and is going to have to make choices. Eventually that is going to filter down into a set of initiatives landing at your door. Then it will be you who has to make them work in the real world. It would make sense therefore if you could see how the various initiatives might work together. You may judge that AOM is great (we hope you do) but that it would be better introduced a little later, or you might say let's get AOM in first and then follow up with Project Z.

Broadly speaking, initiatives are going to come at you from three directions. You might find yourself in one or more of the following three scenarios:

1. Working with consultants (or other change agents) to introduce new methods. These often get branded with imaginative names and are often variations on one of a few themes. They are also, often, very good and will do a lot for your operation so everything we say is intended to support the principles behind these initiatives. At one time, business process re-engineering (BPR) was all the rage, Lean comes in and out of fashion and at the moment Agile is becoming very popular. We will talk about the links between AOM and both Lean and Agile. Don't worry if these are just meaningless words to you; you can come back to the chapter on these (Chapter 18) if your organization starts to look at them.

2. Working with leadership trainers. This is related to the category above but focuses more on the people and culture-based changes. We will talk a little about how AOM relates to leadership programmes and also to the renewed interest in empowerment and self-directed work teams.

3. Implementing new technologies. For some organizations, technology is seen as the key to performance improvement. This is such a vast area and so dependent on the type of operation you are running that we can't really do it justice in the space we have. We will touch on just two technologies: workforce management (WFM) and business process management (BPM).

What the future holds

Chapter 19 will describe some of the key trends in operations: how they are changing the way operations work and how AOM will help you to work through these.

Much of what we have written about so far is based on large numbers of people working together in offices. The people see each other, talk to their team leader, have meetings in rooms and talk about the weekend sport, *Game of Thrones* or whatever. But we know the world is changing. People may choose to (or have to) work shorter hours. They might work only on certain days of the week or for an agency that places them in other people's operations. Technology has helped more people to be able to work remotely and increasingly some aspects of back-office operations work is being replaced by automated processes – popularly referred to as robots although they don't look anything like Kryten from the TV series *Red Dwarf*. (Our editor tells us that those of a more youthful disposition may need to Google this one unless they watch a lot of TV re-runs!)

We will suggest how AOM can play a part in supporting:

- a gig economy where people's time is offered and bought much more flexibly;
- remote working scenarios;
- a world where people work alongside robots.

We understand that many of these changes might be outside of your control and may be thrust upon you. They may feel like opportunities or threats to you, and we can't know how they will play out in your own world. What we are sure of is that the better you are able to 'do the day job', the easier it will be for you to take on board new changes or, better still, have some influence over those changes.

If you are in a canoe in fast-flowing water, it is important to paddle. That gives you some control and the ability to steer. If you don't paddle you are at the mercy of the flow and could end up bouncing off the rocks. We hope that the thoughts in this final part of the book will give you more opportunity to paddle (whatever proverbial creek you might be up!).

Chapter 18
AOM in a world of change

This chapter is going to look at just a few of the other big initiatives that might be on your plate and competing for your attention alongside AOM. We know that you may not have much choice over what the company decides to implement, or when, but knowledge is power and so we will give you what you need to know about how AOM relates to some of the most common initiatives that may be in play where you work. This will help you to see the synergies and opportunities for getting the best out of all that is going on around you.

Lean

If you haven't come across Lean, it is a method of planning and managing production that grew out of work done at the car maker Toyota in the 1950s. 'Lean manufacturing' grew out of this pioneering work and the principles have gone on to be applied outside of manufacturing, which is why there is a very strong chance that Lean has entered your world.

Here is a quick 'bluffer's guide' in case you ever find yourself at a particularly niche dinner party of operations managers.

Championed by engineer, Taiichi Ohno, the Toyota Production System (TPS) was a revolutionary approach to manufacturing that sought to reduce the cost of manufacturing by eliminating any wasteful activity from the process and only doing what added value to the product.

One consequence of the focus on eliminating waste was avoiding the costs associated with making and storing stuff. By making goods on a 'Just in Time' basis, less money is tied up in part-completed products and the costs of warehousing are greatly reduced. As far as we are concerned, the term 'Lean' was originally a reference to not being 'overweight' with lots of unnecessary inventory, and not, as many people seem to interpret the term, slimming down staffing levels.

Probably your first, and often only, contact with a Lean programme would be to produce some flow diagrams of your key processes. You would then have come up with a simpler process by identifying and removing any non-value-adding steps. The hope being that this would cost less to operate and also customers got served more quickly.

You may also have been introduced to the idea of 'failure demand'. This is the amount of work that you must do because something went wrong somewhere else in the process. This includes activities such as writing out to customers because the local branch did not capture all of the information first time or receiving chasing calls from customers whose email had not be responded to. Doing things right first time reduces failure demand and can reduce operating costs.

What has this got to do with AOM?

First off, we should say that we are big fans of Lean where it is well thought through and well implemented. Our roots go back to the same traditions as Lean, but we have placed a different emphasis on where to start when setting about improving performance.

The first big similarity is the focus on the system. We have talked a lot about systems thinking in this book and made it clear that we think performance improvement comes *mostly* from improving the way workflow is organized and managed, rather than by placing an emphasis on individual worker performance, since they are usually constrained by the system in which they are working.

In practice, however, a lot of Lean programmes are not quite as *systemic* as you might expect. Many Lean initiatives often do little more than focus on mapping processes and eliminating non-value-adding steps. Some do go further to look at more fundamentally reorganizing the 'flow' of the operation around customer demand, but we find very few Lean programmes that fundamentally address the question of capacity management. This means that your organization could be 'doing Lean' but not actually touching anything associated with the AOM principles and processes we have been talking about.

It may help if we look back at where the Toyota Production System started and how this has morphed into different disciplines. It seems to us that there were three main levers for change.

1. Improve quality by focusing on designing for quality and getting things right first time. This was characterized by statistical process control back in the day and evolved through the Total Quality movement and on to what is now called Six Sigma.
2. Improve process flow: simplifying processes, removing non-value-adding activities and reducing failure demand. This is where Lean is typically focused.
3. Transforming the production management process: in Toyota and in manufacturing in general, this was characterized by the rise of 'Just In Time' supply and improving the flow of work. This is part of Lean, but it often gets less attention. This is absolutely the core focus of AOM.

AOM's focus on the third element makes it very important in supporting and reinforcing Lean programmes. AOM helps you to extract the benefits from any process simplification and without it there is a risk that any cost savings will exist only in theory, not in practice.

If you remember back to Chapter 3, we talked about fluctuating productivity and latent capacity. We said this is what happens when resourcing is not synchronized with volatile and fluctuating levels of incoming work. This is important because if the only focus of your Lean programme is process simplification then the fluctuating productivity will still be there and it is virtually impossible to capture and use the benefits of any time theoretically released by simplification if it is 'lost in the noise' of an uncontrolled management system. AOM will help to synchronize work and resource, reduce the noise and help you focus on delivering the benefits.

Agile

At the time of writing, Agile is springing nimbly from its roots as a project management approach in software development, out though into wider fields of project management and on into all sorts of areas of production management: both in manufacturing (not our thing now) and in service operations (very much our thing). We would be most surprised if your organization hasn't looked at Agile as a means of delivering some performance improvement. If it hasn't arrived with you yet, here is the lowdown on what you need to know and how AOM and Agile share many common features.

The discipline of Agile was generated as an approach to software development and has been credited with dramatically improving the efficiency and effectiveness of the process. Despite the fact that actual empirical evidence of Agile's success is limited, it has caught the imagination of the business world and the method is now being applied to projects other than software development and is increasingly being seen as a philosophy for management more widely.

So, as fans of a good method, what do we think about Agile? Is it worthy of the hype? Will it help to transform service operations like yours?

In short, our answer is this: *Agile is great. If that is the banner under which you want to optimize the performance of your operation, then it is a sound place to start.* The values of self-organizing teams, emphasizing adaptability over long-range planning, and pulling work on a 'just in time' basis are all positives. (Did you spot that 'just in time' phrase again?

Yes, Agile, like AOM, draws from the same well as Lean did, and they all go back to systems thinking and the Toyota Production System.)

We didn't mention it above, but we now need to mention *Kanban*. This is a Japanese word meaning a card or visual sign. Taiichi Ohno used these in Toyota as a way of moving production through the factory. Kanban was the mechanism used to make Just in Time work in factories and has become commonly used in Agile programmes to refer to the display of short-term work requirements.

Agile comes from the world of computer programming so if service operations are going to make the best of Agile, they will have to adopt and adapt – not just copy blindly. Just as software developers have adapted the language of Kanban from Toyota car manufacturing principles and applied it to project management, service operations will have to make further adaptations – and these will have to be made in a way that shows a fundamental understanding of the principles of service operations.

In our view, Agile proposes a good set of principles. Its exponents will have the same challenge that we have had for years: how to turn common sense into common practice and how to make good, intelligent disciplines the default option that is easiest for an organization to follow for the long term. Whether your organization talks about Agile or active management, many of the principles are the same.

How do AOM and Agile principles compare?

Agile has lots of principles, more than we need to discuss here, and the 12 principles of the Manifesto are very project focused. (For example, the first principle is: 'Customer satisfaction by early and continuous delivery of valuable software,' which kind of gives away the roots of the method.) Here are a few of the well-known principles that you will need to be aware of, and which will help you orient Agile to AOM.

1. Adaptive vs predictive

Agile favours an adaptive approach, with rolling waves of short-term plans. Like AOM, Agile works on the basis that over-reliance on forecasting can stifle responsiveness – hence our joke about forecasts being lucky or wrong. Both disciplines place more emphasis on being able to respond to customers' changing needs and not just trying to predict them.

Allied to this is the principle of decentralizing planning and moving control as close as possible to the customer. This is key in Agile and you will have read that this is what we adopt in AOM. It is not always common practice in service operations, many of which still rely on top-down command and control. Just like AOM, Agile challenges this command-and-control approach to service operations.

2. Short-interval feedback

This principle comes from systems thinking and reflects the needs for complex systems to have good feedback loops if they are to stay in control. We haven't got bored with saying that yet and hope that we have shown that this is necessary in service operations. Agile comes at this from the world of computer programming where it has been realized that it is better to work in short 'sprints' than to run the whole marathon and present the complete programme to the customer only to find they have changed their minds. If you are trying to do Agile in your operation, look at what we have written here about planning and control feedback loops. In that sense, AOM is Agile for service.

3. Visual controls

Short-interval feedback is often best achieved through visual controls. In the original manufacturing environment, this could be taken quite literally: the empty bin, the Kanban card etc. In projects and operations, the data is often distilled into tables and charts but these are kept simple and visual by putting them up on displays or whiteboards for the whole team to see. We have described some of these sorts of controls for AOM in Part 3. These reduce the cycle time to report and respond and help to create the sense that the outcome is everyone's responsibility.

4. Stand-up meetings

Agile favours short meetings – with stand-up meetings often preferred as a way to emphasize their short and dynamic nature. This review of short-term progress and commitment to the next steps is key to Agile and is a great discipline in service operations. This is something we support through AOM and it is another reason why it is important to empower team leaders and put them in control of the planning process on behalf of their team. If planning is too centralized then these planning meetings become little more than top-down communication sessions.

5. Cross-functional/multi-discipline team working

Agile emphasizes self-organizing teams, where the team's constituents represent the right group of people to carry out the specific tasks. Teams will form and re-form as required over the lifetime of the project. This is great if it can work for you and your teams, but we have seen the idea of self-organizing teams get misinterpreted in the world of service operations. What seems to happen is that 'self-organizing' gets interpreted as 'independent' and the barriers between teams go up rather than come down and silos become isolated. Everything we have been saying about load balancing between teams is really important for optimizing performance. So here is a way AOM can help you to be Agile: it can help break down the silos and keep resources flowing to where the work is.

Agile or active?

More than 20 years ago, we chose the word *active* to represent our approach to operations management. At the time, we wanted to reflect the notion that team leaders should be actively involved in delivering high-performing teams – not passively passing on commands from above. We differentiated active management from reactive management – which was all about firefighting and just solving the immediate backlog or overtime problems. We also used active management to differentiate from bureaucratic management – which was all about setting long-term plans and structures and just following the rules.

On reflection, the principles of active or Agile management are very much the same:

- Move control as close to the customer as possible.
- Have the team leader work as a servant to the team, working out short-term priorities and using instant feedback to optimize performance in the moment.
- Create clear and visible information systems that engage team members and make it easier for everyone to take responsibility for performance; then widen the notion of the team so that teams can collaborate to deliver the best outcomes for the customer and the operation.

We believe that our key insight was to realize that principles were not enough; that exhorting a certain set of behaviours would not necessarily deliver those behaviours. Agile, or indeed active, management may be largely a culture change, but you need a practical method, as outlined in Part 3 to drive and sustain the change.

Of course, the nature of your organization's Agile programme may not be up to you but there is a strong chance that you will be in the hot seat for making it work. Everything you have read in this book will help you to be Agile, if that is what your company wants. As we see it: *if you want to be Agile, get active.*

AOM and leadership

We are going to touch on two popular initiatives that you may well come across and both are linked to leadership in different ways. If your organization is doing any leadership initiatives, this bit will help you to see how AOM still fits in, and supports, these kinds of changes.

First, we want to talk about culture change and leadership training. Here, the emphasis is on how leaders, like you, make a difference through inspiring peak performance in the people who work for them. Second, we will talk about empowerment and self-organizing teams. You may see references to 'self-managed teams' or 'leaderless teams' but don't worry, we think your job is perfectly safe for the time being.

Leadership programmes

We have worked with several great leadership trainers and consultants over the years and one of the best we have seen is called PlanetK2. The founder, Keith Hatter, has written a very good book called *Perform*. PlanetK2 come from a sports psychology background and they argue that leaders should set about developing performance at work the same way coaches develop elite athletes. If you get a chance to work with these people, jump at it. Even if you haven't been exposed to something as structured and insightful as PlanetK2's offering, there is a good chance you have been on one or two leadership courses, and a lot of organizations will see this as the key to unlocking the potential of their front-line employees.

We have had potential clients say to us something along the lines of: 'Never mind all that AOM planning stuff, all we need is great leaders to get the best out of our people.' Okay, so that might be a sale we didn't make, but our argument would be that great leadership is necessary, but it is not sufficient. It comes down to something we keep going back to: leadership is just one part of the system. Change one part of a stable system and it risks becoming unstable and out of control. Make complementary changes to all parts of the system for real, lasting results.

A lot of this book has talked about behaviours and has stressed the role of leader as coach. We absolutely believe that great leadership helps to make great organizations. Two points from our discussions earlier in the book are particularly relevant here.

First, remember Performance = Willingness × Ability × Opportunity? Great leadership can create more willingness. You can create a 'performance culture' if you like, but the *opportunity to perform* will be limited unless work is planned and managed effectively. You still must do the balance sheet and match workload and resources to optimize productivity. Otherwise you will only have an underachieving team of potential high performers.

Second, remember *Behaviour, Method, Skills, Tools*? The four parts of AOM. All of these have to come together and be complementary to really achieve success.

Perhaps the biggest problem we have seen with leadership programmes (even great ones) could unkindly be called the 'flash in the pan' phenomenon. The programme works superbly well and achieves great results but within a year or two it all seems to have been forgotten.

A client of Neil's who deals in contingent labour supply (temps and suchlike) went through a leadership programme and saw a leader from that time talking to a colleague a year or so later. They were describing how they had been taught to fold T-shirts in one exercise to illustrate the value of having a method. After a few moments of the colleague looking bewildered, the enthusiastic manager telling the story dwindled to a halt mumbling, 'Well, I guess you had to be there…'

And this is the point: many leadership programmes work very well on the people who attend, but the messages and culture don't last as people move on, get promoted, focus on other things. This is where AOM can help. You know that AOM is based on sound leadership principles and it also provides explicit behaviours and a coherent method to make sure that those leadership values are lived and breathed every day. Since the AOM methods will outlast any one generation of leaders, the benefits of leadership training will be constantly reinforced and will also last much longer.

Empowerment

This is another initiative that you are very likely to have to play a part in. When we talk about empowerment, we are not talking about just giving employees some choice over swapping from the morning to the afternoon shift; we are talking about new organizational designs that place more of the decision making that is traditionally thought of as 'management' within the team. You may hear of this under terms such as self-organizing, self-managing or even leaderless teams.

It generally means changing the responsibilities of managers, rather than losing large swathes of people who had 'manager' in their job title. The shift tends to be towards coach and co-ordinate and away from command and control – something we have mentioned quite a few times in this book.

Do self-managed teams need AOM? The answer is definitely 'yes' and the clue is in the word 'managed'. Teams may not have a leader or manager as such, but they still need to manage their own environment rather than just fall victim to it. Some self-managed teams will continue to have a resource co-ordinator who effectively does the work of planning and balancing work and resources on behalf of the team. That person would attend loading meetings to trade work and resources with other teams and that person would take responsibility for spotting trends, doing the double-loop learning and helping the whole team to be the best it could be. Other teams might share out or rotate those duties. Either way, you are likely to still have a role in co-ordinating the people or representing their teams. It would be naive to try to run an operation without doing these things.

Wherever we have seen operations try to create entirely self-sufficient teams, they have simply created a bigger problem of small sub-optimized silos that have no means of talking to each other. In our view, AOM represents one of the best vehicles for working towards self-directed teams, if that is your company's ambition. AOM gives common language and common purpose that will make it easier for senior management to step out of the way, confident that teams will have a framework for working together.

Our recommendation to you, as a department manager, is to use AOM to shift the emphasis from team leaders being 'in command' to have them be 'in service' to their teams. If your organization goes down the route of creating self-managed teams then you will be well on your way, and your role as architect of the future operating model will be assured.

AOM and other technologies

All the principles and disciplines of AOM are embedded into our own cloud-based technology called Workware™. It is one of several technology solutions that are commonly referred to as workforce management (WFM). Whether you get the chance to use Workware™, create your own spreadsheets or use another technology, if you get involved in the choice over the tools you can use, there are a few things to put on your checklist. Make sure that the tool:

1. supports a coach-and-co-ordinate culture, not just command and control;

2. focuses on being more adaptive than predictive;
3. helps to move control as close to the customer as possible, making it responsive (like the reflex action before the central nervous system kicks in);
4. encourages the removal of silos, creating real co-operation across barriers, between teams;
5. supports double-loop learning and hence continuous improvement.

We will deal with just one other technology that you will almost certainly have in your own office. This is the *Business Process Management Suite*: the tools that help to design, analyse and automate steps in a process as work moves through the operation. In the next chapter, we will talk about the rise of the robots, or more accurately the automation of processes, but here we will deal with the evolutionary level before that, which is where you are most likely to be at. We are talking about workflow technologies: the tools that help capture work, put it in queues, present it to workers to process, and then capture data and move the work on to the next task in a process.

This probably sounds familiar. Most operations have something like this and they may think that it is managing the work, so they don't need something like AOM on top of this. Maybe that will one day be the case, but we have yet to see a technology that moves work through the process stages and simultaneously seeks to balance capacity to demand. The workflow tools rarely extend beyond the core processes to, say, find in-house development work to do that wasn't in the plan to keep everyone busy, or maybe discussing priorities between different core operations functions because all are overloaded.

We have talked about these things in this book: the loading, commitment and variance meetings; trading resources; being responsive to changes in customer demand; learning lessons to drive continuous improvement. This is what AOM is all about – workflow technologies will help with some of this, but are not going to do it for you. You will still have to design and include these sorts of activities into your operation, over and above what you get from your workflow tools.

Much of this might change when you switch the lights out in your office because all the people have left and the robots don't need to see what is going on. We will look at how likely that particular vision of the future is in the next chapter.

Chapter 19

AOM and the future of operations

Now could be seen as an exciting time to be working in operations, or just bewildering. The chances are your job is different today than it was a year ago, and you are probably already trying to get your head around the next set of changes. Technology isn't just speeding things up or automating them; it is fundamentally changing the way work gets done. If you find that half of your workforce actually works for agencies, who supply you with your labour needs, what does this do to your resource planning? And how do you engage and motivate people if they are employed by someone else? If many of your people are working from home, how do you make sure they are performing well? And how do they know how well they are doing compared to their colleagues if they never see them? If all your workers are robots, what are you for? Do you need to be replaced by a mechanic with an oil can?

The changes that will be happening around you, even to you, may be huge and we wouldn't want to minimize them but we would like to reassure you that the skills that probably got you to where you are today (organizing and managing people) will continue to be relevant for the foreseeable future. Even if half of all operations work were done by robots, that would still leave millions of people to be managed, and supported in learning to get along with their robot colleagues. It is also likely, if history repeats itself, that for almost every routine job that gets automated away, new and different jobs will arise that require the human touch. People ain't done yet.

AOM's people-focused approach that emphasizes optimizing the complex, human, system will remain relevant into the future. In this chapter, we will assess AOM against three big changes that are almost certainly happening in your world right now. These changes are:

- the growth of the gig economy, with more people being required or choosing to work for themselves and then only being paid for the time they work;
- remote working, where people don't congregate in large offices in the way they once did;
- the rise of the robots; as robotic process automation, artificial intelligence (AI) and machine learning change the nature of many information-based clerical jobs, just what is the role of the human worker?

These changes are not ones you can control, and in some ways are societal, not just organizational. It would be easy to say: 'That's all way above my pay grade.' But, as we said in the previous chapter, the best you can do is to 'paddle the canoe'. AOM is designed to help you to take some control, grasp the opportunities and minimize the threats.

Let's dive into the future.

The gig economy

It is tempting to associate the gig economy with some very significant negatives such as zero-hours contracts, where people are only paid for the work that they do, even if they can't make use of any of the time between working. There are also issues around the lack of employment security and weaker rights than other employees. But there is a different and more positive side to consider.

Gallup, the American analytics and advisory company, has gathered and presented a lot of interesting data about the future of work. Here are a couple of statistics from Gallup:[1] over a third (36%) of workers in the US participate in the gig economy in their primary or secondary job and nearly two-thirds of those (64%) say they prefer this working arrangement. That clearly leaves many people who aren't happy, and we should note this, but the model does seem to be working for a lot of people.

Gallup make an interesting distinction which is relevant to us working in operations like banks, insurance companies and other back offices. They distinguish between *independent* and *contingent* gig workers. Independent gig workers are those who find work through online platforms or are independent contractors, while contingent gig workers are temporary and on-call workers often provided by an agency to operations who are seeking for fill gaps in their resourcing. It is highly likely that more of your workforce will be contingent gig workers, supplied by agencies in the future. This can give greater flexibility, but here's the thing: independent gig workers feel they have a good work–life balance, some independence and freedom while contingent gig workers are far less positive.

Gallup compared what they call 'traditional workers' (that is, people on the pay roll working for one company), independent and contingent workers on several aspects. Below are a few highlights that are relevant to us in the context of AOM.

When Gallup asked these three categories of worker how they felt about different features of their job, such as having a healthy work–life balance, a feeling of belonging in the workplace and having some autonomy/authority, independent gig workers generally responded the most positively.

---

[1] S. McFeely and R. Pendell, 'What workplace leaders can learn from the real gig economy', *Gallup*, 16 August 2018. Available from www.gallup.com/workplace/240929/workplace-leaders-learn-real-gig-economy.aspx [accessed 27 August 2020].

- The only category where traditional workers were the most positive group was on the matter of 'being paid timely and accurately'. On the other hand, traditional workers were the least positive group when it came to saying they were paid fairly or that pay motivates them.

- Contingent gig workers were the least likely to say that they felt a sense of belonging in their workplace, felt passionate about work or that they had any stability or security.

- Both contingent workers and traditional workers responded least positively on questions about being involved in goal setting, having any control over performance metrics and receiving feedback.

It seems that some of the challenges that companies have in engaging and inspiring traditional workers are as difficult or more difficult when employing contingent workers. So far, we have tried to show how AOM creates a more positive and engaging culture that would address some of the concerns that Gallup raises about how traditional workers see their world. We would say that AOM will be even more important in a world with more contingent workers.

Gallup make two suggestions to help you to better manage traditional workers and also get the best out of using contingent workers:

1. Redesign traditional jobs to have more of the benefits of independent gig work, such as more flexibility, autonomy, respect and regular feedback. All of this is the aim of AOM and is what we have been promoting throughout this book. AOM helps by:
   a. getting people out of their silos and working across teams;
   b. moving control closer to the customer so that workers have greater autonomy;
   c. treating people with respect (on a Theory Y basis) and creates regular feedback through the planning and control process.

2. Train managers better to relate to their temporary workforce. Communicate mission and values to these workers and engage them as you would all others. AOM helps you to engage contingent workers by:

    a. giving them clarity over the contribution they make in delivering the operation's goals;
    b. providing supportive data on how they are performing in a consistent framework alongside the 'traditionally employed' workers;
    c. creating a more stable and predictable working environment that will help contingent workers to feel like a positive part of the operation, and not just a 'panic purchase' to cope with a crisis.

Remote working

According to Gallup,[2] 43% of US workers work off site for at least part of their time, and a majority of workers would choose to work from home in preference to a small pay rise. With technology making it easier than ever both to route work to remote workers and to stay in touch with these workers, we are likely to see increasing levels of remote working. The 2020 Covid-19 crisis also forced a lot of service operations to consider remote working on a much greater scale and we have seen some operations adapt very well while others have clearly struggled. How did this affect your management of capacity and drive for the best possible levels of performance? Did the pandemic create a 'new normal' for you?

Many of the issues that we talked about in the context of gig workers apply here as well: the need to create a sense of belonging, engagement

---

[2] A. Hickman and I. R. Levey, 'How to manage remote employees'. *Gallup*, 14 August 2019. Available from www.gallup.com/workplace/263510/manage-remote-employees.aspx [accessed 27 August 2020].

and feedback are even more important in workers who may not see or interact with co-workers on a frequent basis. We are separately high-lighting this group of workers partly because of the unique nature of working largely in isolation, but also because we have concerns over the direction of travel for managing this group. The same computing power that is enabling home or remote working is also driving data centred (rather than person centred) performance management, and this is problematic.

There are technologies that can monitor every minute of a worker's day, every keystroke they make and even everywhere they go. With such access to data, there is a temptation to manage-by-monitoring. Some data-capture companies will even go so far as to argue that you can make employees work harder by making sure they know they are being watched. Even if this were true (and it definitely is not), surely the aim of management is to recruit, develop and retain people who want to do their best, not to develop mechanisms to force reluctant people to work harder?

One of our performance coaches was working with an outsourcing client a while back and noticed how agents had found a sneaky way around what they felt was intrusive monitoring. These agents all had dual monitors but the 'screen scraping' technology used to track their activity only worked on the primary monitor. As a result, the agents would run their 'monitored' process on one screen while doing as they pleased on the other. On closer investigation, our coach found that the agents weren't necessarily on social media or such like on the second screen. No, they would be updating other records, or checking on process advice, operating standards and suchlike, which helped them do their job but were not recognized by the system.

It seemed a shame to our coach that agents' ingenuity was being put into beating the system rather than serving the customers because they were being given no real motivation to do so. In this case, as in many others, the simple removal of some of these 'Big Brother' mechanisms led to improved productivity.

Please don't misunderstand us on this point: since line-of-sight management is impossible with remote workers, it makes perfect sense to have technology to help capture data on what is going on. It is just that there is a greater risk of reliance on remote performance monitoring to deliver improvement. Hopefully, we have made it clear that operations cannot monitor their way to peak performance; they have to manage their way there, so how can AOM help to manage remote workers?

- AOM methods support good time management. This leads to treating remote workers as individuals with realistic targets for the work they can get done in the time they have available. Work can hang oppressively over the home worker outside of their committed hours. Time management is important so that remote workers 'leave work, switch off, and go home' even if they have been working on the kitchen table.

- One problem with home working can be the inability to see what others are doing. Just as some aspects of social media are causing people to believe that everyone else is more attractive, more contented and having a better life than they are, so too there is a risk of home workers believing the everyone else is working harder and achieving more. AOM will help them to set realistic targets for themselves. It is also hard, if you are at home, to know that everyone in the office is running around in a panic because the recent floods have sent the inbound insurance claims through the roof. The visibility of AOM's planning and now-expected methods will help home workers to have more sense of the context. This will help if they are suddenly asked to do more or work on tasks that they don't normally have to do.

- There is a danger that managers will feel the need for intrusive monitoring technology to keep a check on remote workers. While automatically capturing data can be helpful in allowing workers to get on with serving customers, using software in a way that implies you don't trust people could backfire. By creating a common language, AOM makes it easier to talk about what needs to be done and who is doing what. 'Here's what we need you to do and we trust you to get it done' is a much more positive message than 'We're watching you...' AOM can help managers to build trust with remote workers, rather than relying on Big Brother to try to do their job for them.

If you have remote workers as part of your teams, then the things we have talked about in this book will be relevant for you. All of the activities, such as planning, loading meetings, commitment meetings, daily huddles and variance analysis, can be run remotely via file sharing and/or conference calling. They are all opportunities to engage with remote workers and help them to feel, and to be, less remote.

The rise of the robots

Let's be clear: when we talk about robots we are not talking about human-like machines who are doing the same work as humans, but just don't need toilet breaks. When we talk about robotics in the back office of service operations, we are really talking about the automating of some of the processes currently done by people: entering data, moving it between systems, doing calculations, and suchlike. Strictly speaking, this is robotic process automation (or RPA), but referring to robots is becoming a common shorthand.

It is happening now, and it is not just the odd experiment here and there any more. We have seen some hundreds (out of many thousands) of jobs among our client operations be replaced by RPA technology.

While this has led to some job losses and cost savings, it has been much more common for clients to take the opportunity to get the people who have been freed up to do more for customers and to do more of the things that people are really good at.

There is certainly no doubt that RPA is making waves in the press at the moment with predictions ranging from the over-blown 'end of work as we know it' to the prosaic 'increasing efficiency by 35% in areas where RPA is adopted'. Some notable people have even gone so far as to suggest that machines now really do represent a threat to humanity: Stephen Hawking warned that artificial intelligence could be the end of mankind.

Behind the hype is the reality that more and more work is being done by machines, and that for the foreseeable future it is not a question of either machines or people doing the work, it is a fact that people and machines will work alongside one another. The real issues we should be addressing are therefore not about the end of work as we know it (or indeed humanity) but about how to organize and manage these two very different capabilities together.

Systems thinking tells us that we should consider the knock-on effects of any single change that we make in an organization. That way we avoid the law of unintended consequences. Introducing RPA into your operation could have profound effects on your people, the work they do and how you have to behave as a manager. Get it right and everyone wins. Get it wrong and short-term gains could give way to long-term cynicism and bad press.

Here are four issues for you to chew on. When it comes to you managing a team of robots alongside your current carbon-based life forms, we hope the following thoughts will help you.

Implications for human talent management

RPA inevitably targets some of the simpler, more repetitive work that is currently done by people in the back office. Indeed, this is often heralded as a human benefit as it takes away the drudge work, leaving people the opportunity to do more interesting and challenging work.

This may well be true but we also need to consider the potential changes to the mix of people working for you:

- Take away the third of employees from the lowest pay bands and your average wage bill goes up. You will have a smaller, more highly paid workforce.
- Similarly, the average educational requirement may well go up as staff are focused more on exception handling, problem solving and human contact.

A better-paid, higher-educated workforce will bring challenges of its own. You may find it harder to recruit or keep the best resources as competition grows more highly skilled people. Your key workers may feel they have a stronger bargaining position. There may also be a general rise in people's expectations of the way they are managed.

For some time now, the world of operations management has been in two minds over how best to improve operations performance. On the one hand, there has been a continuing trend for decades to emphasize employee engagement, wellbeing and the power of good leadership. (The kind of stuff we have been writing about in this book.) On the other hand, the increasing availability of data and computational power has led, in some operations, to a return to old-style centralized 'command-and-control' management. Technology that captures and uses data to improve performance is often classified as workforce optimization technology. It is dominated by tools that support the centralization of planning and the removal of initiative from front-line leadership. In some operations, people have been treated like machines, or just numbers in a spreadsheet: a mathematical challenge to be 'optimized'.

AOM bridges that divide between human-based performance improvement and mathematically based technologies. As you have seen, we do use numbers and we do propose to plan and schedule work, but we do it in a way that understands people, their motivations and what it takes to get the best out of them. The robots may not need your best motivational speech on a Monday morning but their capacity does need to be actively managed. Manage the robots by the numbers and use the numbers to create the space for people to be the best they can be.

Making the RPA business case

Where would you start if you had to make a case for adding 'robots' to your team (or to challenge a business case that was being put to you)?

There are countless examples from management history where technology changes have been only partially costed and justified by only looking at local savings without considering the wider implications. Once again, we know this might be outside of your current level of control, but if you get involved in RPA projects then it is worth having this bit of context.

One problem with the business case for robots can be the starting point. If a part of your operation is inefficient, how should you measure the benefit of automating it? There may be big cost savings to be made by automating it, so the case is compelling. But if you ran a one-off project to make the operation more efficient first, the savings to be made would be less, and the case for the robots may no longer be so strong.

Our message to COOs (which we hope you will tell them!) would be 'don't automate inefficiency'. Not just because it flatters the automation business case, but because there is also a danger of 'locking in' inefficient processes. RPA may allow you to do something more quickly; being inefficient quickly is unlikely to be a recipe for long-term competitive advantage.

RPA commentators we have spoken to all stress the need to precede RPA implementations with good process analysis – indeed, one of the benefits of initiating RPA work is that it can help an organization to take a long, careful look at its processes. Getting the management process right (in other words, 'doing AOM') prior to automation is, in our view, equally important.

Blended planning

It is likely that for the foreseeable future, if you have RPA, it will exist as part of a blended workforce. In some places, the robotic capacity will sit alongside human capacity doing very similar work with one or the other acting as the surge capacity. More often, the robotic capacity will take on one or more elements of a process, sitting within a process flow with work passing back and forth between human and robotic capacity.

Remember our discussion at the start of this book about latent capacity, and how productivity varies because work volumes are often highly volatile? Our research has shown that this is just as true for 'robot workers' as it is for human workers. Some days, the robots are very busy and living up to their business case; other days, half of them are just humming in the corner, doing nothing. (Can robots get robo-bored?) This is an issue if the business case for the robots assumed a certain level of utilization. Robots may be cheaper to run than people, but paying them while they do nothing is still a waste of money. We have found that the principles of creating a balanced plan apply just as much to a blended human/robot workforce as they do to a fully human one.

This will present you with some very interesting planning challenges. Here are just a couple to think about for now.

1. *Bottleneck scheduling.* You could be faced with some quite complex planning challenges when some of your resources are robots. For example, one 'robot' breaking down (and they do!) might mean you need to find ten people to cover the work. Also, the robots might do one stage of the work very quickly but just cause it to pile up behind the next process along. There is a whole field of operations management dedicated to optimizing planning when processes take very different times to complete. We can't go into it here but it is called bottleneck scheduling and you may need to find out more about this at some point in the future.

2. *Blended scheduling.* So far, we have generally seen operations that introduce robots also introduce parallel planning, with technicians doing capacity planning for the robots and team leaders (or planning teams) doing the same for the people. We are also seeing this gradually evolve into a single role. So far, the AOM method has coped with planning 'robots' and people side by side. Trust us, when you get to manage robots, everything you have learned here will still apply.

RPA in operations management

So far, we have been talking about RPA as a means of automating the work in the office and what it might mean for the way work is managed, but what about your own role? Could the robots be about to take that over? If anything, we think the real revolution in front-line operations management will be the continued trend away from 'command and control' and towards 'coach and co-ordinate'. Increasingly, the role of team leaders and department managers will be to organize the complex world that people work in to help them to focus on being the best they can be. Your job is safe if you care about people and are passionate about developing and inspiring others.

That is not to say AI can't help you. This is another form of advanced computer programming that is often lumped into a trio of robotics, artificial intelligence and machine learning.

We are already adding AI elements to our planning software. Our aim is to make it as quick and as easy as possible to 'do the maths' so that you can focus on supporting the people. Here are a few of the ways that AI technology could help with operations management:

- Providing forward forecasts of work and resources and highlighting problems to managers.
- Analysing trends or highlighting variances, and presenting choices to managers.
- Presenting data in intuitive and meaningful ways to help managers to communicate with staff.
- Creating rapid and meaningful feedback to individual staff members to help them to manage and improve their own performance – improving engagement and intrinsic motivation.

While it might help you, or your team leaders, to do some of the necessary calculations, or help to review trends, identify variances and so on, real managers will still be the best placed to manage real people. Another notable statistic from Gallup is that managers account for at least 70% of the variance in employee engagement scores, with engagement being strongly linked to productivity.[3]

Until back offices are completely 'lights out' operations, with all work being carried out by robots, the real world will contain a blend of people and robots. This will raise the requirement for great leadership of a more confident and capable workforce.

---

[3] R. Beck and J. Harter, 'Managers account for 70% of variance in employee engagement', *Gallup Business Journal*, 21 April 2015. Available from https://news.gallup.com/businessjournal/182792/managers-account-variance-employee-engagement.aspx [accessed 9 September 2020].

Perhaps one of the greatest hopes for the rise of RPA is that – as we manage the robotic capacity alongside people – operations will stop treating people like machines and rediscover the art of leadership, and more people will be managed and supported 'the AOM way'.

Chapter 20

Goodbye and good luck

We started out saying how tough it can be being a manager in service operations. Little could we imagine just how tough. As we write this conclusion, we are in lockdown in the 2020 Covid-19 pandemic. This has meant personal tragedy for many and economic challenge for just about everyone. If you were working through the crisis, we hope that you, your family and colleagues were spared the worst and that things are better now.

Like everyone else, we have witnessed many small acts of kindness and seen just how flexible and innovative people can be in the most difficult of times. More than ever, we believe that trusting people and giving them the opportunity to be the best they can be is the single best way to run operations. One of the main messages in this book has been that you should plan on what you know and then respond to what changes. Some changes are bigger than others, but what we have learned recently is that the principles of AOM – being flexible and responsive, empowering teams to take more control over their own work, and breaking down silos so that everyone can 'win together' – really do matter.

We finish here with a short summary to help you on your way.

- You work in service operations. While lessons can be learned from other sectors, look out for solutions that are designed with service in mind, rather than adaptations from elsewhere. Look back at the four '-ilities': intangibility, inseparability, perishability and volatility, and ask how any solutions that are proposed to you will measure up to the things that make service the unique challenge that it is.

- Remember that most operations have latent capacity. This is time that you can get your hands on and put to good use if you adopt the right sort of approach to planning and managing capacity. That capacity is there for the taking. Not because your people are letting you down but because the systems that they work in and that dictate the way they work are often letting *them* down. You are in a position to improve the systems and help your people to perform as well as they can.

- There are no magic bullets. Be wary of anyone who tells you that one solution is going to answer all your needs. No piece of technology, no one project will solve all your problems. Think about your operation (the whole thing, or just the bit that you manage) as a *complex, human system* and remember the rise of the cane toads. *Complex systems* need solutions that understand and take account of the interactions between all parts of the system if you are going to avoid unintended consequences. *Human systems* need to be understood in human terms: motivation, politics, hope and fears are all real and legitimate things to think about when making changes.

- AOM addresses the operation as a system by having a four-part approach. It describes a set of behaviours for leaders (and the skills to support those behaviours) that will help you to achieve the best possible outcomes. AOM also prescribes a standardized method (and tools to make that method easy to do) which helps everyone to work in the same way and follow the same leadership behaviours. The key words to describe the kind of behaviour that we are talking about is active management. This involves planning ahead and then constantly using information to gain feedback in order to learn and improve.

- Active management goes hand in hand with a Theory Y style of management. It is a style of management that believes the best of people and seeks to bring that out. (As opposed to Theory X, which believes the worst of people and seeks to overcome it.)

- The AOM method involves a simple cycle of *Forecast* (what you expect to happen), *Plan* (what you intend to do), *Control* (using feedback to achieve the best outcome) and *Review* (to learn lessons and do even better next time).

- To make the method work, you need to have a common currency. Just as you can't add up pounds and dollars without converting them to the same unit, neither can you add together all your different service tasks without first converting them into the common currency of time. This common currency helps you to be fair to everyone and to plan work and time in a way that means you can give people the opportunity to perform well, and then get out of their way and let them do it.

- Don't get too hung up on forecasting. Forecasts are generally lucky or wrong, and it can be very liberating to let go of the (often) false certainty of complex forecasts and accept that your real skills, and greatest contribution, lie in being able to respond, learn and adapt. Develop your people and design the ways they are working actively to respond to change.

- Planning involves adding up the time required to do all the work and comparing it to the time available. This involves accounting for not just the work for the customers but also all the important internal stuff such as training. Any given team could have too little or too much time to do the work required. For this reason, balancing the load between teams is an essential activity. Nobody wins unless everybody wins.

- Control comes from extracting information from a sea of data. Use critical comparisons to help you. These involve comparing: actual outcomes to planned outcomes, actual outcomes over time (to look for trends) and actual outcomes to agreed standards (to make sure that your assumptions still hold good). Making comparisons in good time gives you the greatest opportunity to adapt and achieve the best possible result. Making comparisons visible to all helps to focus everyone on playing their part.

- Think about the Review element as a process of learning lessons. This requires an open acceptance that errors are made. Look for lessons, not people to blame. We recommend double-loop learning. The first loop involves doing everything you can to perform well within a given set of assumptions; the second loop involves asking if those assumptions still stand or if they should be modified.

If you follow the above advice, you will be able to teach your teams to build simple, meaningful, plans. You will be able to hold loading meetings that will help all your teams to pull together to realize the best possible outcome for all involved. Your team leaders will be able to run commitment meetings with their teams to engage and motivate them, and then they will be able to produce now-expected plans so that they deliver the best possible outcome as their plan unfolds. Finally, you will be able to run variance meetings with your team leaders to help them learn lessons and do even better next time.

Do all of the above and you will find that your life becomes easier. Your teams will hit their targets more often while seemingly not having to work so hard. Panic followed by inactivity will be a thing of the past and a smoother, more even rhythm to your days, weeks and months will become apparent.

As the AOM operating rhythm beds in, you will be best placed to take on all the new challenges that are likely to come your way. As you find it easier for your teams to stay on top of business as usual, you will find the time, and mental space, to deal with new projects, new technologies, social changes and whatever else the world of service operations has to throw at you.

Thank you for taking the time to read about AOM. We hope that you will benefit from the ideas we have presented and we wish you the very best for your future in operations. If you haven't already done so, please continue your journey with us by visiting your online toolkit at https://activeops.com/aomtoolkit.

Acknowledgements

As much as we'd like to claim that everything is this book stemmed from our own unique insight and inspiration, the truth is that we have had a lot of help and inspiration from others along the way. Only the errors and omissions can we fully claim to own.

It was Tony Paris who first introduced us to the idea of active management through his simulation training. Tony is a genius at creating simulations and we have used his model of a back-office operation to train many thousands of people. Much of this training was done while we were partners in the Organization Consulting Partnership (OCP) and we owe a debt of thanks for the opportunity we had to explore and develop our approach to operations management while working with this top-draw team of consultants. They also backed us to approach Jon Soar of Iconics, who took the risk of building the very first version of our Workware™ software on a profit-sharing basis.

While working at OCP, we were lucky enough to have Eagle Star as a client and we are grateful to Roger Townsend for taking a punt on us and our newly minted software. Roger has continued to be a friend and business mentor to us for many years but it was that first opportunity to load up a dozen or so floppy disks into his team leaders' desktops that really got us started. (Yes, it was a while ago!)

In the early days, a few notable individuals helped us to introduce AOM to clients around the world, travelling many thousands of miles. Charles Cawthorne, Bob Sime, John Jones and Giles Slinger all played a big part at the start. As did Ian Carter and Oliver Cunningham. We should give a special mention to Paul Moroney, the 'third founder' of ActiveOps. He had the courage and foresight to set up the first AOM franchise for our products in Australia, and has been a pivotal figure in the growth and development of the company from its outset. He was also one of the first to read and improve the early drafts of this book.

We have learned a lot from every client we have worked with over the years and many 'early adopters' saw something in our concepts and technology that convinced them to take a bet on us. A bet we believe has delivered great business returns every time, but we nevertheless appreciate the act of faith. While the clients are too numerous to mention, we do want to make special reference to Nigel Adams who was the operations leader at National Australia Bank when we first took our wares to that continent. Nigel has continued to believe in us and support us as his career developed.

We have benefitted from always being surrounded by a great team within ActiveOps. We cannot name all the current and past employees, but you know who you are and we thank you. With a specific role in helping us get this book over the line, we are grateful to Shany Elkarat for project management and to Peter Cregg for reviewing the later drafts.

Most recently, a number of people have been kind enough to carry out a 'beta read' of our final draft and have given us some great insights which have improved the book that you have before you. We are grateful to Amanda Jones, Westpac; Anshuman Tiwari, DXC Technologies; David Murfet, National Australia Bank; Gemma Carter, SS&C/DST; Harald Hoeve, Rabobank; and Whitney J. Sherman, Fifth Third Bank.

Finally, as is traditional, we would like to thank our spouses Diane and Sue for putting up with us throughout the whole journey that has got us to this point. You have kept us going during the difficult times and kept us grounded.

About the authors

Neil has been helping organizations to improve their front-line operating performance since the late 1980s. Originally qualified in Psychology, he started work at Lucas Industries in the 1980s, gaining experience in manufacturing production management, learning about systems engineering and the Toyota Production System. Neil went on to work at PA Consulting Group, focusing on culture and organizational change in financial services and the public sector.

Richard qualified in Systems and Management at City University London, researching and applying technology support for decision-making processes based around John Warfield and Peter Checkland's system thinking theories. Working at PA Consulting Group and Coopers and Lybrand, he specialized in organizational change management and operational effectiveness in financial services.

Together, Neil and Richard began developing the Active Operations Management (AOM) method and the Workware™ software as partners at the boutique consultancy OCP. They launched ActiveOps as an independent business in 2005.

Today, Richard leads the business and Neil sits as a non-executive member of the board.

About ActiveOps

Since its inception in 2005, ActiveOps has grown from being a six-person operation based in Reading, UK, to become a global operation with divisions in Australia, India, South Africa and North America.

ActiveOps proprietary software and embedded AOM methodology helps organizations, and the individuals within them, to transform the confidence with which they plan work and capacity.

The company's goal is to simplify managing operations: delivering better outcomes, lower stress levels and greater wellbeing for all involved.

Around the world, millions of working hours, and many millions of work items, are forecasted and planned for; and then managed and reported upon using ActiveOps software and method.

The solution is successful because it delivers consistency of outcome, speed to benefit and sustained results over the long term.

Everyone in ActiveOps really cares that clients achieve the results they require and expect.

Printed in the USA
CPSIA information can be obtained
at www.ICGtesting.com
JSHW012014140824
68134JS00025B/2421

9 781788 602310